National Park Service
U.S. Department of the Interior

Water Resources Division
Natural Resource Program Center

Technical Report NPS/NRWRD/NRTR-2006-346

ASSESSMENT OF COASTAL WATER RESOURCES AND WATERSHED CONDITIONS AT WRANGELL – ST. ELIAS NATIONAL PARK AND PRESERVE, ALASKA

Eran Hood, Ginny Eckert, Sonia Nagorski, Carrie Talus

I0438869

Cover photos:

Top Left: Malaspina Forelands, Matt Jones
Top Right: Malaspina Forelands, Molly McCormick
Bottom Right: Tyndall Glacier (Icy Bay), Eric Veach
Bottom Left: Malaspina Foreland, Molly McCormick

The National Park Service Water Resources Division is responsible for providing water resources management policy and guidelines, planning, technical assistance, training, and operational support to units of the National Park System. Program areas include water rights, water resources planning, marine resource management, regulatory guidance and review, hydrology, water quality, watershed management, watershed studies, and aquatic ecology.

Technical Reports

The National Park Service disseminates the results of biological, physical, and social research through the Natural Resources Technical Report Series. Natural resources inventories and monitoring activities, scientific literature reviews, bibliographies, and proceedings of technical workshops and conferences are also disseminated through this series.

Mention of trade names or commercial products does not constitute endorsement or recommendation for use by the National Park Service.

Copies of this report are available from the following:

National Park Service   (970) 225-3500
Water Resources Division
1201 Oak Ridge Drive, Suite 250
Fort Collins, CO 80525

National Park Service   (303) 969-2130
Technical Information Center
Denver Service Center
P.O. Box 25287
Denver, CO 80225-0287

Assessment of Coastal Water Resources and Watershed Conditions at Wrangell – St. Elias National Park and Preserve, Alaska

Dr. Eran Hood[2], Dr. Ginny Eckert[1], Dr. Sonia Nagorski[2], Ms. Carrie Talus[1]

Technical Report NPS/NRWRD/NRTR- 2006/346

[1]Biology Program
[2]Environmental Science Program
University of Alaska Southeast
Juneau, AK 99801

January 2006

This report was prepared under Task Order J9W88 04 0016
of the Pacific Northwest Cooperative Ecosystem Studies Unit (agreement CA90880008)

WATER RESOURCES DIVISION

National Park Service - Department of the Interior
Fort Collins - Denver - Washington

TABLE OF CONTENTS

List of Figures

List of Tables

List of Appendices

Acknowledgements

We would like to thank numerous people for their help in the preparation of this report. Mason Reid, Devi Sharp, Eric Veach, and Cody Murphy provided information about the park. Edwin Knuth at the University of Alaska Southeast GINA lab created the original maps for the report. Jeff Sloss from Discovery Southeast provided information about recreational use in coastal WRST. Mark Flora, Cliff McCreedy, Jim Tilmant, Eric Veach, Barbara A. Cellarius, and Kristen Keteles at the National Park Service provided input throughout preparation of this report and extensive comments on the draft report, which greatly improved the final product.

Commonly used abbreviations

ADEC – Alaska Department of Environmental Conservation
ADFG – Alaska Department of Fish and Game
ADNR – Alaska Department of Natural Resources
ANILCA – Alaska National Interest Land Conservation Act
ATV – All Terrain Vehicle
EMAP – Environmental Monitoring and Assessment Program (of the US Environmental Protection Agency)
EPA – US Environmental Protection Agency
GOA – Gulf of Alaska
HAB – Harmful Algal Bloom
NADP – National Atmospheric Deposition Program
NOAA – National Oceanic and Atmospheric Administration (US Department of Commerce)
NPDES – National Pollutant Discharge Elimination System (of the US Environmental Protection Agency)
NPS – National Park Service (US Department of Interior)
NWI – National Wetlands Inventory (of the US Fish and Wildlife Service)
POPs – Persistent Organic Pollutants
PSP – Paralytic Shellfish Poisoning
UAS – University of Alaska Southeast
USDA – US Department of Agriculture
USFWS - US Fish and Wildlife Service (US Department of Interior)
USGS – US Geological Survey (US Department of Interior)
WRST – Wrangell-St Elias National Park and Preserve (National Park Service Designation)

Executive Summary

Wrangell-St Elias National Park and Preserve (WRST) is located in southeastern Alaska, bordered on the south by the Gulf of Alaska and on the east by the Canadian border. The park and preserve is the largest unit in the National Park System consisting of over 5 million hectares of mountainous terrain with an extensive area of icefields and glaciers. WRST was established by the Alaska National Interest Land Conservation Act (ANILCA) in 1980. The purpose of the park is to promote ecosystem integrity through carefully planned public use and to provide for a variety of uses including: subsistence hunting and gathering, scientific investigation, interpretation of natural forces, the inspiration and solitude of wilderness experience.

The focus of this report is the coastal water resources within and around Wrangell-St Elias, which consist of both freshwater and marine ecosystems. The coastal region of WRST stretches from Icy Bay to Yakutat Bay and consists of approximately 1.9 million acres (768,906 hectares) located along 125 miles of coastline on the Gulf of Alaska. This remote coastal area, although largely glaciated, is ecologically rich containing nearly 1000 acres (404.69 hectares) of intertidal communities and abundant wetlands and coastal streams. Coastal WRST is an important migratory route for numerous bird species and contains spawning areas for salmon, steelhead and Dolly Varden.

Coastal water resources are critical from the standpoint of both biological integrity and human utilization of national parks. The diversity and quality of freshwater and marine habitats determines the distribution of plants and animals within the park and provides aesthetic and recreational opportunities for park users. The purpose of this report is to provide a comprehensive assessment of the current condition and possible impairments, both natural and anthropogenic, of water resources in the coastal region of WRST. The report inventories coastal water resources and reviews their conditions based on currently available data and information. In addition, the report identifies gaps in data and information that hinder the assessment of water resources and provides recommendations for future monitoring and mapping of coastal water resources.

The coastal region of WRST is extremely remote and thus human utilization of the region has been relatively sparse. The closest community to coastal WRST is the town of Yakutat (population 800) located across Yakutat Bay from the Malaspina forelands region of the park. Yakutat serves as the base of operations for this region of the park and contains the District Ranger Station. Unlike in interior regions of WRST, mining in the coastal area has been extremely limited. The coastal forelands are used for subsistence hunting and trapping for animals such as bear, goat, harbor seal and a variety of birds. Airplanes are used by subsistence users to access the coastal region of the park and ATVs are used to access some private inholdings in this area. In addition, the WRST coastline is used for both commercial and recreational/subsistence fishing. Tourism is limited, however flightseeing, sea kayaking, and hiking are becoming more popular in areas like Icy Bay and Yakutat Bay.

The climate of coastal WRST is dominated maritime air from the Gulf of Alaska and is characterized by significant precipitation and relatively moderate temperatures. The Gulf of Alaska is dominated by a persistently-located area of low pressure known as the Aleutian Low. This area of low pressure generates powerful winter storms, which routinely produce >15 m waves and gale strength winds. The Aleutian Low oscillates in strength and location throughout the year but maintains its influence on the regional climate of coastal WRST. There are not permanent climate stations within this region of WRST, however Yakutat has a mean annual temperature of 39.3°F (4.06°C) receives an annual average of 141.5 inches (359.41 cm) of precipitation. Coastal areas of the park can receive more than 8 meters (26.25 ft) of snowfall annually.

The coastal region of WRST encompasses two large fjords, Icy Bay and Disenchantment Bay as well as the coastal forelands at the toe of the Malaspina Glacier. Greater than 90% of coastal WRST is covered by glaciers and icefields. As a result the hydrologic regime of coastal watersheds is dominated by glacial runoff. The coastal water resources in WRST include: glacial and clearwater rivers and streams, lakes and ponds, wetlands, glacial ice and permanent snowfields, and groundwater. WRST does not contain nor have jurisdiction over any marine waters within its boundaries, however coastal and intertidal resources in and around park boundaries are discussed in this report. The outer coast of WRST borders the Gulf of Alaska, which contains more then 12 % of the continental shelf holdings of the US.

Coastal WRST supports a wide range of flora and fauna. Harbor seals inhabit the coast and have pupping grounds in Disenchantment and Icy Bays, sea otters populations occur discontinuously along the park's coastline and several species of porpoise and whales have been identified. The park is one of the most important migratory bird pathways in southeastern Alaska and supports populations of murrelets, gulls, and eagles. Sampling for fish in Yakutat and Icy Bays in 2001-2002 identified 31 species of fish. Coastal WRST contains 1,000 acres (404.69 hectares) of intertidal habitat, however very little is known about intertidal flora and fauna. Glacial rivers and streams within WRST tend not to be highly productive due to high levels of suspended sediment, however many streams along coastal WRST support populations of anadromous fish such as king and silver salmon.

Water quality in coastal watersheds and coastal areas of WRST is not monitored. Due to the remote location and low level of human activity, it is assumed that water quality within the coastal areas of WRST is in good condition (Table i). Limited gravel mining has occurred along Independence Creek in Icy Bay and NPS field survey of water quality at this site in 1989 provides limited information on basic water quality parameters such as temperature, pH, dissolved oxygen, metals and conductivity. All of the parameters measured in this survey fell within normal ranges set by the EPA and the State of Alaska. A Water Resources Scoping Report conducted by the NPS Water Resources Division in 2003 provides a comprehensive overview of water quality in WRST, however this report contains no information on water quality in coastal streams. Similarly, no studies of groundwater resources have been carried out along the coastline of WRST.

Several water quality impairments have been identified in the area of coastal WRST. The Colorado Oil and Gas Corporation drilled two wells and established a warehouse along Sudden

Stream in Yakutat Bay. Soil and surface water around the site were found to have elevated levels of barium and chromium and the site was remediated in the early 1990's. In addition the wells mentioned above, the Alaska Department of Environmental Conservation has listed two logging camps near the park boundaries in Icy Bay as contaminated sites because of high levels of heavy metals in groundwater at the sites. Although there is currently no mining or petroleum drilling in coastal WRST, there are 13 offshore exploratory petroleum wells along the park coastline west and southwest of Icy Bay.

Petroleum spills present a clear environmental risk to coastal water resources in WRST (table i). There are a variety of potential sources for petroleum releases within park boundaries including: marine vessels in near-shore areas, small aircraft and associated fuel storage facilities, ATVs, and historic drilling sites and storage areas. In particular, an accident involving a tanker or barge hauling hazardous material could have disastrous effects for coastal ecosystems. Several sites in and around WRST currently have Geographic Response Strategies (GRS), which are specific spill response plans for sensitive areas created by the Alaska Department of Environmental Conservation, however there is currently no such plan for the Icy Bay area.

Coastal WRST like many pristine high-latitude areas is currently at risk from atmospherically derived contaminants (Table i). Mercury and a group of chemicals known as Persistent Organic Pollutants (POPs) are the two primary contaminants of concern for Alaska. Levels of these pollutants have not been monitored in coastal WRST, however sediment cores collected in nearby Glacier Bay National Park indicate that rates of mercury deposition in the area have been rising consistently since the Industrial Revolution. In addition, a study of sea bird eggs in the Gulf of Alaska found elevated levels of POPS.

The Gulf of Alaska is a major shipping route and the area around coastal WRST sees traffic from commercial, sport, and subsistence fishing vessels as well as water-bourne tourism. Marine vessels have the potential to impact coastal water quality by a variety of mechanisms including: the accidental release of petroleum, the release of wastewater or other discharges, and the resuspension of sediments. In addition, there is concern that underwater noise from marine vessels may impact the behavior and communication of marine mammals along the WRST coastline.

Harmful algal blooms are known to cause paralytic shellfish poisoning (PSP) and Alaska has one of the highest incidences of reported PSP in the world. Since 1973, there have been 176 incidences of PSP in Alaska from 66 outbreaks, with the majority in Southeast Alaska. Little is known about the distribution or abundance of PSPs in coastal areas of WRST (Table i). The Alaska Department of Environmental Conservation (ADEC) is responsible for testing shellfish for PSP, however shellfish are only tested for PSP in association with a commercial harvest or mariculture facility. More information is needed in order to evaluate if HABs are an issue of concern in WRST, and any unusual incidences of mass mortalities of marine bird, mammal, and fish populations should be suspected as possible HAB-related events.

Non-indigenous aquatic invasive species that have been introduced or are moving into Alaskan waters include multiple species of fish, plants, and invertebrates. Pathways of introduction that could affect coastal WRST include: fish farms, aquaculture, transport on or in ballast water from ships or fishing vessels, live seafood trade, and sport fishing gear. A variety of invasive species have been identified in marine environments in southeastern Alaska, however there has not been a comprehensive survey of invasive species in coastal WRST (Table i).

In coastal WRST, ATVs are used to access some private inholdings, additionally some individuals ride ATVs below the mean high tide line which is outside of the unit boundary and under the jurisdiction of the State of Alaska. A 1997 study of ATV use along the Malaspina forelands found that vehicular traffic was having little impact on coastal ecosystems. ATV use in interior areas of WRST has previously been associated with impacts such as shifts in species composition, decreased cover of plant species, the melting of permafrost, and accelerated erosion.

There are several natural hydrologic and geomorphic processes that pose a threat to coastal water resources in WRST including land surface uplift and the advance of the Hubbard Glacier in Disenchantment Bay. Currently the land surface along the WRST coastline is being uplifted at as much as 12-24 mm yr^{-1} as a result of the unloading of ice from the earth's crust since the Little Ice Age. This uplift is altering the landscape of coastal WRST and causing dramatic changes in fisheries and wildlife habitat including shifts in the composition and location of vegetative communities. Continued uplift also has the potential to alter the hydrology of small coastal streams by causing a decrease in the elevation of the local water table relative to the land surface.

The Hubbard Glacier located in Disenchantment Bay has created a dam at the entrance to Russell Fjord twice in the last 20 years and is currently re-advancing across the mouth of the fjord. Flooding events associated with the creation of a glacier dam across Russell Fjord have the potential to dramatically alter the physical landscape of the Yakutat forelands and pose a threat to valuable fisheries in the Situk River as well as the road system and airport for the town of Yakutat. The US Forest Service, the National Park Service and the US Geological Survey have an ongoing research and monitoring program on the Hubbard Glacier.

Climate change is an important natural resource issue for national parks in Alaska, and recent research suggests that changes in climate may dramatically impact water resources in Alaskan parks (Table i). The most obvious effects of climate change on hydrologic resources in Alaska are changes in the extent of permafrost, snow cover, glaciers, and sea and lake ice cover. Currently, glaciers in coastal WRST are thinning at rates as high as 4 meters per year. An important hydrologic effect of increased glacier melt is an increase in runoff from glaciers, which can lead to the creation of new streams, and alter sediment, streamflow, and temperature regimes in surrounding streams. It is also likely that climate change is affecting lakes and ponds within the coastal region of WRST. The area of small lakes and ponds within in WRST has decreased dramatically since the 1950's, with unknown effects on the species populations dependent on these waterbodies.

Recommendations for addressing data gaps and establishing baselines are discussed on pages 50-53 of this report.

Table i. Potential for impairment of coastal WRST water resources.

Indicator/Stressor	Upland/ Freshwater	Estuary	Marine/ Intertidal
Water Quality			
Eutrophication	OK	OK	OK
Contaminants	PP	OK	PP
Hypoxia	OK	OK	OK
Turbidity	OK	OK	OK
Pathogens	OK	OK	OK
Habitat Disruption			
Physical benthic impacts	OK	OK	OK
Coastal development	OK	OK	OK
Altered flow	OK	OK	OK
Erosion/Sedimentation	OK	OK	OK
Altered salinity	NA	OK	OK
Recreation/Tourism usage	OK	OK	PP
Other Indicators/Stressors			
Harmful algal blooms	NA	OK	PP
Aquatic invasive species	PP	PP	PP
Impacts from fish/shellfish harvesting	PP	OK	PP
Terrestrial invasive species	OK	OK	OK
Climate change	PP	PP	PP
Land surface uplift	PP	NA	NA

Definitions: EP= existing problem, PP = potential problem, OK= no detectable problem, shaded =limited data, NA= not applicable.

A. Park Description

A1. Background

A1a. Setting

Wrangell-St. Elias National Park and Preserve (WRST) is located 200 miles (322 km) east of Anchorage and 120 miles (193 km) northeast of Valdez, Alaska (Figure 1). WRST spans approximately 13.2 million acres (5.3 million hectares), is the largest national park in the US, and contains the continent's largest assemblage of glaciers and peaks above 16,000 feet (4877 meters). The Park comprises 8,147,000 acres (3,296,974 hectares), and the Preserve consists of 4,171,000 acres (1,687,944 hectares). Additionally, there are over 700,000 acres (283,280 hectares) of private, state, native and university lands inside the park boundaries. A total of 9,660,000 acres (3,909,263 hectares) spread throughout the Park and Preserve of WRST are designated and managed as Wilderness– the largest in the US National Park system. WRST has four mountain ranges, the Chugach, Wrangell, St. Elias, and Mentasta/Nutzotin Mountains and includes lands along the Gulf of Alaska coastline, the eastern half of the Copper River drainage, and the Yukon drainage of the Nabesna, Chisana and White Rivers. The focus of this report is the coastal region of WRST which consists of approximately 1.9 million acres (768,903 hectares) along the Gulf of Alaska (Figure 2).

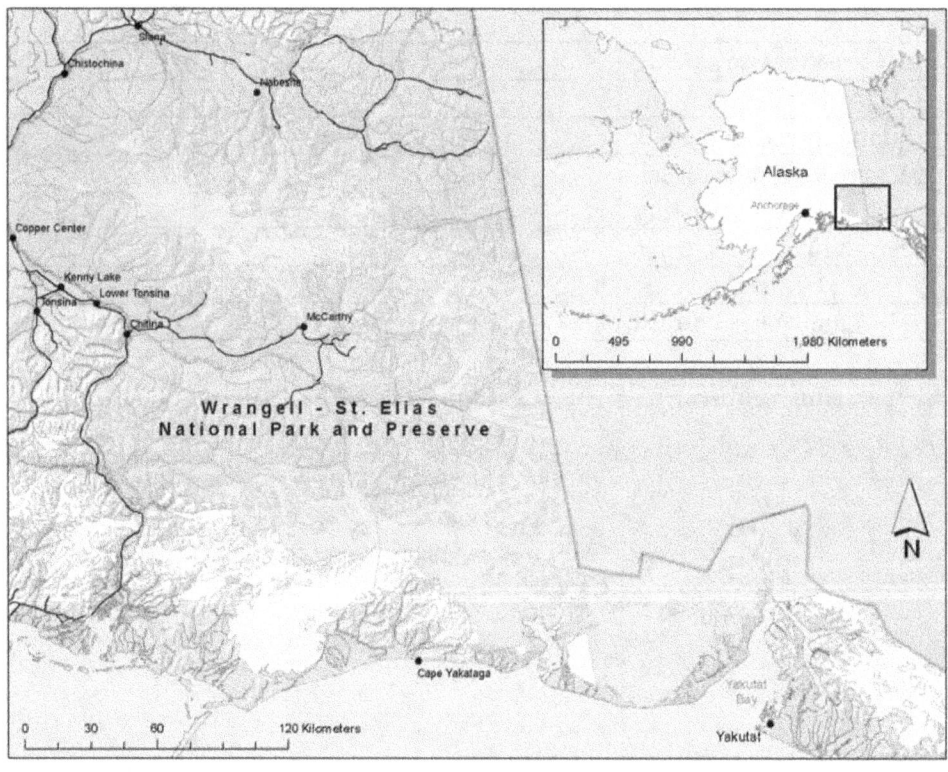

Figure 1. Location of Wrangell-St Elias National Park and Preserve within Alaska

6

WRST was established by the Alaska National Interest Land Conservation Act (ANILCA) in 1980, and as a result, many activities that are not traditionally allowed in a national park, such as subsistence use of fish, wildlife, and firewood, are allowed in the Park, and subsistence and sport hunting are allowed in the Preserve. ANILCA grants access for these activities by snow machines and motorboats. In addition, over 700,000 acres (283,280 hectares) of private, state, native and university lands are located inside WRST boundaries and are used for commercial and residential development, logging, and mining (Weeks 2003). These factors create a unique challenge for the NPS in managing the ecosystems in WRST.

The coastal zone of WRST extends from Icy Bay to the west to Disenchantment Bay to the east and includes the upper reaches of Icy Bay, the Sitkagi Bluffs in the Malaspina forelands, all of the coastal areas of the Preserve, the western side of Yakutat Bay, and the western and northern portions of Disenchantment Bay (Figure 2). WRST has over 125 miles (201 km) of coastline and 1,000 acres (405 hectares) of intertidal communities (Weeks 2003), which support a wide diversity of algae, invertebrates, fish, marine mammals, and birds. Coastal lakes and streams supply spawning grounds and habitat for anadromous and non-anadromous fish species, many of which have important commercial value for the region. The Yakutat coastal zone, which extends from the eastern boundary of the WRST coastal zone, is considered to be the most important habitat for bird migration in Southeast Alaska (Patten 1981). Yakutat (population 800) is located across Yakutat Bay from WRST and is the base of operations for the coastal portions of WRST, containing the District Ranger Station.

Glaciers dominate the land area in coastal WRST. Large glaciers along the coastline of WRST include the Guyot and Yahtse Glaciers flowing into Icy Bay, and the Turner, Vallerie, and Hubbard Glaciers flowing into Disenchantment Bay, and the Malaspina Glacier, which does not presently reach the sea. These glaciers are part of the largest connected glacier and icefield complex in continental North America. Additionally, the Malaspina Glacier, which is the largest glacier along the coastline, is approximately the same size as the state of Rhode Island and, with an area of ~5,000 km^2 (1,931 square miles) contains the largest piedmont (unconstrained by topography) lobe of any temperate glacier (Molnia 2001; Sauber et al 2005). The Malaspina Forelands stretch along the base of the Malaspina Glacier and are a relatively flat, narrow coastal strip between Icy Bay and Yakutat Bay. Coastal glaciers are dynamic and are largely responsible for shaping the structure of the coastline. These glaciers also feed a large network of rivers and streams that transport tremendous quantities of freshwater to coastal marine systems.

During the past 200 years, many glaciers along the coast have retreated, leaving bays along the Gulf of Alaska. For example, the multi-armed and 30-mile (48 km) long Icy Bay became exposed only in the past century as the result of the rapid retreat of the Guyot, Yahtse, and Tyndall Glaciers. Glacial action continues to affect the coastal bathymetry and geomorphology in WRST. Sediment inputs from calving tidewater glaciers and subaerial meltwater streams deposit massive volumes of sediment in coastal embayments such as Icy Bay and Yakutat Bay. Sedimentation rates in areas of these bays have been shown to exceed 1 meter per year (3 feet per year) and the resulting sedimentary structures are responsible for substantial shoaling (Molnia et al 1979, Jaeger and Nittrouer 1999).

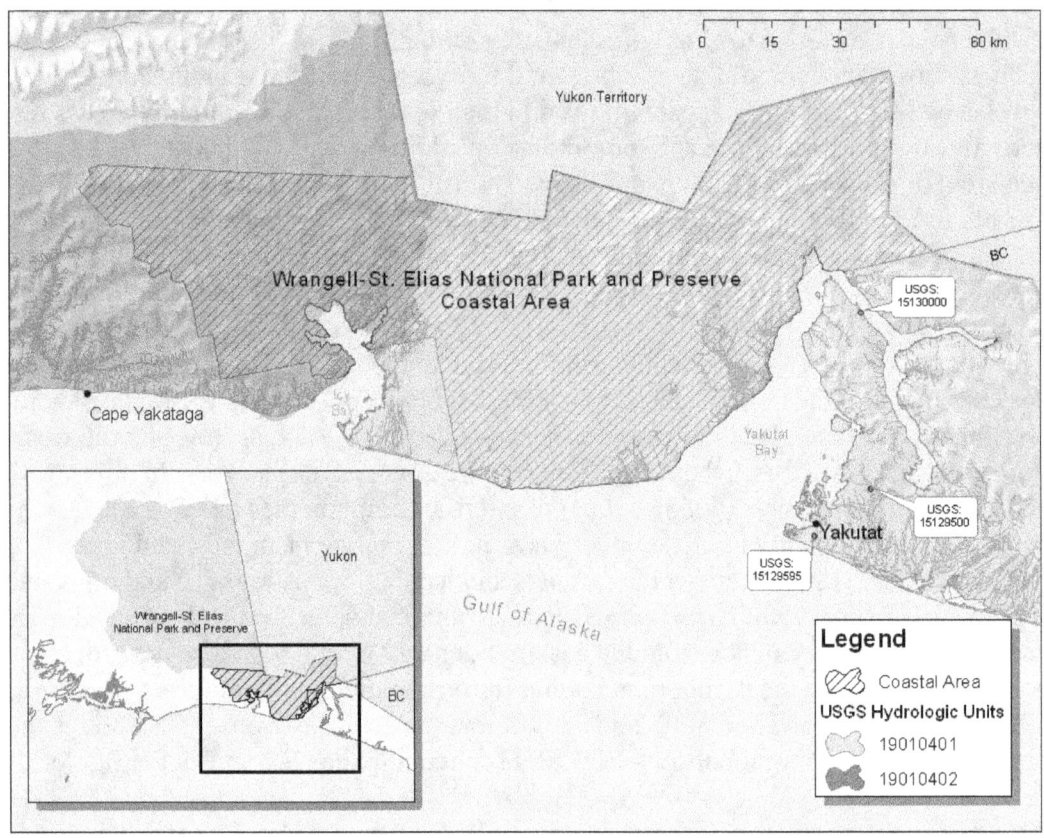

Figure 2. Coastal region of WRST, which is the subject of this report. The US Geological Survey defines two hydrologic units in the coast region of WRST: Yakutat Bay (19010401, in yellow) and Bering Glacier (19010402, in blue). Also shown are three active USGS stream gages in the vicinity of WRST.

A1b. Human utilization

For thousands of years, Native Alaskan peoples have lived and subsisted through traditional hunting, fishing and gathering in the coastal area of WRST. These people trace their origins to a number of different homelands. The native people in coastal WRST are considered to be the northernmost group of the Tlingit, the group populated much of coastal Southeastern Alaska. However, Alaska Natives from inland regions have also been assimilated into the coastal populations (Mills and Firman 1986). Inland peoples that migrated into the area include the "...Eyak of the Copper River and the Ahtna from Chitina..." (Mills and Firman 1986). Also, the southern Tutchone of the Upper Yukon and Alsek Rivers moved into the area by means of the Alsek River corridor that transects the Saint Elias Mountains and flows into Dry Bay (Mills and Firman 1986). Along the coastal zones of the park, Tlingit peoples traditionally hunted harbor seals in both Disenchantment Bay and Icy Bay, and seals are still an integral part of the modern Tlingit subsistence diet (Mills and Firman 1986).

Before Russian contact, there were numerous Native Alaskan villages along the coastline, particularly along coastal rivers. These villages were strategically located to support fur

8

trading between inland and Southeast Alaska Native groups. Russian fur traders arrived in the region and became considerably active in fur trading with the people along this coast. One consequence of this influx of Russian traders was that most Native communities were devastated by diseases introduced by the Russians. Many of the survivors of these disease outbreaks migrated to other areas or eventually settled in Yakutat (de Laguna 1972).

Although many gold miners came to the WRST mountains in the early 1900s, most mining activity occurred inland and did not substantially impact the coastal area of WRST. However, prospectors did come to the coast and many lived in Yakutat (Mills and Firman 1986). The late 1800s and early 1900s were prosperous times for the Yakutat area due to commercial fishing and the abundance of salmon in the area (Mills and Firman 1986). However, by the end of World War I through the 1950s, the population of human inhabitants in the area reached an all time low as a result of a crash in salmon stocks (de Laguna 1972). Oil exploration began out of Yakutat in the 1950s and 1980s, and commercial logging and road construction brought many people to Yakutat in the 1960s (Mills and Firman 1986).

Recent surveys of Yakutat residents show that approximately 50 percent of the population is of Native Alaskan heritage (Mills and Firman 1986, US Census Bureau 2000), and traditional land rights and subsistence activities remain important to many Native people in Yakutat. People continue to hunt on the WRST coastline for bear, moose, goat, harbor seal, and birds such as ducks, geese, and seabirds (Betts et al. 1999). The WRST coastline is fished commercially and non-commercially for salmon and halibut (Betts et al. 1999).

Mills and Firman (1986) surveyed 50 randomly selected households in Yakutat in 1984 to find out harvest quantities and location information for more than 150 different resources taken historically and at the time of the survey along the WRST coastline. Historically, seal camps were established near tidewater glaciers of Icy Bay and Yakutat Bay in the spring when seals congregated on icebergs. More recently, Yakutat residents hunt seals throughout Yakutat Bay, especially near the Hubbard Glacier, in Disenchantment Bay, at the entrances to major salmon producing streams along the Yakutat Forelands, and in Icy Bay. Black and brown bears were traditionally hunted along the Yakutat Forelands but today are usually only hunted along the shoreline of Yakutat Bay and Russell Fjord during the spring when bears are feeding on beach greens and roots. Sockeye salmon run on most rivers of the Yakutat Forelands in the summer. Coho salmon are taken along the Manby shore, and the Yahtse River near Icy Bay. Non-commercial fishing occurs in Malaspina Lake and the coastal waters of Yakutat Bay. Commercial fishing areas include the Malaspina Forelands, the Yahtse River, and Yana stream near Icy Bay. The Yakutat Forelands and Malaspina Forelands are where people hunt for moose, depending on the health of the moose population. Historically, goats were hunted by inhabitants of numerous small villages scattered along the coastline, and more recently, goats are harvested from cliff areas near Icy Bay. Trapping for fur bearers, including mink, marten, river otter, wolf, hare, beaver, lynx, wolverine, coyote, weasel and squirrel, occurred along the coastal area of the Malaspina Forelands south of Sitkagi Bluffs and the shoreline southeast of Icy Bay. Birds, including willow ptarmigan, Canada geese, white fronted geese, whistling (or tundra) swan, sandhill crane, and snipe are traditionally harvested in open wetlands and coastal areas throughout the Yakutat and Malaspina Forelands. Waterfowl, including mallard, green winged teal, pintail, harlequin, old squaw, canvasback, goldeneye, scaup, bufflehead, shoveller, and widgeon, are hunted near ocean sloughs, lakes, and protected ocean waters and the open flats near the mouths of rivers in Icy Bay, Yakutat Bay and the Malaspina Forelands, including the Malaspina Lake area.

Icy Bay, Disenchantment Bay, and Yakutat Bay are experiencing increased recreation and tourism, including camping, hiking, kayaking, flightseeing, and visitation by cruise ships. The first known kayak trip to Icy Bay took place in 1984, and now there are at least seven commercial trips per year (ADNR 1995; personal communication, Jeff Sloss, Alaska Discovery, 2005). The beach landing strip at Kageet Point in Icy Bay is the primary access for the area, in addition to anchorage and staging facilities at Kageet Point, Moraine Bay and Riou Bay (ADNR 1995). Camping, hiking, and wildlife viewing take place at Karr Hills and Kageet Point (ADNR 1995). Kayak trips with Alaska Discovery, one outfitter to use Icy Bay, consist of paddling the length of Taan Fjord and camping near the Tyndall Glacier (personal communication, Jeff Sloss, Alaska Discovery, 2005). The use of Icy Bay for tourism and recreation is likely to increase. Visitors come to Disenchantment Bay to view wildlife such as puffins, shorebirds, and harbor seals. Cruise ships enter Yakutat Bay to view Hubbard Glacier. A public use cabin owned by NPS on Esker Stream gets occasional use by the public, although exact numbers of users have not been compiled recently (personal communication, Cody Murphy, Yakutat District Ranger, Wrangell – St. Elias National Park and Preserve, 2005). The Malaspina Forelands are accessed primarily by airplanes landing on the beach or by boat. Although a permit is required, the Malaspina Forelands are the only area in Wrangell-St. Elias National Park that can be accessed for subsistence purposes using an airplane.

A limited amount of scientific research also takes place in coastal WRST. Recently, a great deal of effort has been focused on understanding the advance of the Hubbard Glacier and the potential consequences of the glacier blocking Russell Fjord. Researchers also use Icy Bay for projects on harbor seals, marine birds, geology, cadastral surveys, and bathymetry.

A2. Hydrologic information

A2a. Climatic setting

Climate in the coastal region of WRST is strongly influenced by the Saint Elias Mountain range and exposure to moisture-laden air from the Gulf of Alaska and is characterized by significant precipitation and moderate temperatures. Yakutat, which is located on the coast at the southern end of coastal WRST, has a mean annual temperature of 39.3°F (4.1°C), and mean monthly air temperatures range from 25.2°F (-3.8°C) in January to 53.8°F (12.1°C)in July (Figure 3). Precipitation peaks in fall when the climate is dominated by onshore flows from low pressure systems in the Gulf of Alaska (Patten 1981). At Yakutat, mean monthly precipitation ranges from less than 6 inches (15 cm) in June to more than 20 inches (51 cm) in October, with an annual average of 141.5 inches (359.4 cm) of precipitation (Figure 3). The coastal region of WRST has intermittent snowpack near sea level and continuous snow cover at elevations above 300m (984 ft) during winter and early spring. Snowfall occurs mainly from November until March with an average annual depth along the coast from 310 to 866cm (122-341 inches) (Patten 1981).

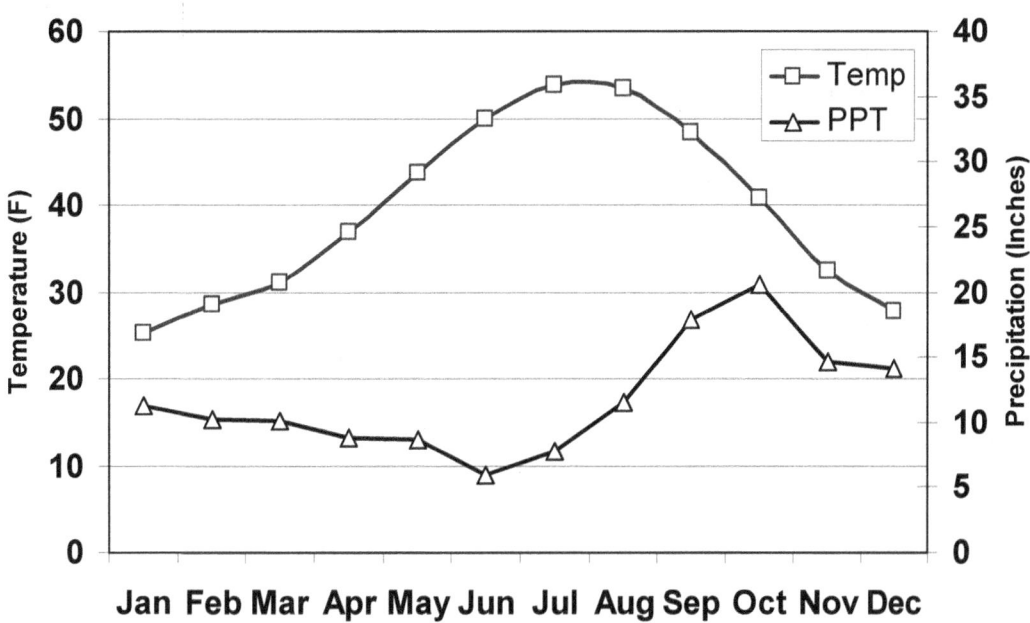

Figure 3. Monthly mean precipitation and temperature in Yakutat, Alaska for 1949-2004. Data from NOAA climate database (http://pajk.arh.noaa.gov/cgi-bin/searchClimData?station=Yakutat).

A2b. Hydrology

The coastal region of WRST encompasses two large fjords, Icy Bay and Disenchantment Bay, as well as a large area of coastal forelands along the Gulf of Alaska. Twenty-five percent of the total landmass in WRST is covered by glacier or permanent snowfield (Weeks 2003), however in the coastal region of WRST this number increases to ninety-two percent. The US Geological Survey defines two hydrologic units in the coast region of WRST: Yakutat Bay (19010401), which contains four streams with active stream gauges, none of which are located within the boundaries of WRST, and Bering Glacier (19010402), which does not contain any active stream gauges (Figure 2).

The hydrologic regime of coastal watersheds in WRST is dominated by glacial runoff, and most streamflow occurs in summer months when glacier- and snowmelt are at a maximum. The Alsek River, which empties into the Gulf of Alaska approximately 100km (62 miles) southeast of Yakutat, provides a representative hydrograph for glacial rivers in WRST. Discharge on the Alsek is closely correlated with air temperature and demonstrates more than a 2000% change in discharge between winter low flows and peak flow during mid-summer months (Figure 4). The coastal portion of WRST also contains a limited number of non-glacial, clearwater streams, which are fed by precipitation and groundwater. Ophir Creek on the Yakutat forelands provides a representative hydrograph for the clearwater systems in coastal WRST, which closely follows seasonal shifts in precipitation with low flows in the spring and early summer and high flows in the wetter fall months (Figure 4).

11

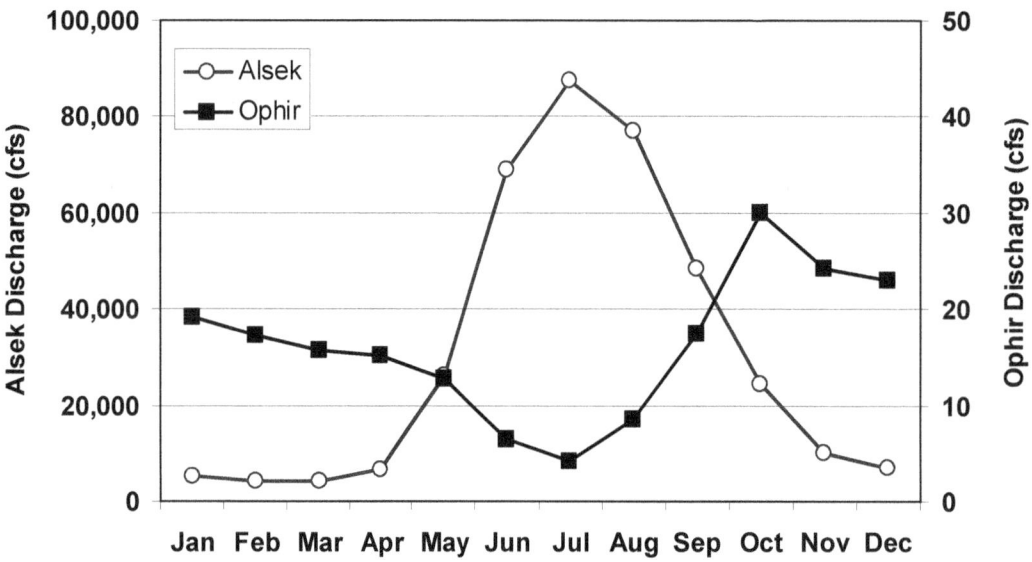

Figure 4. Monthly mean streamflow for the Alsek River and Ophir Creek
near Yakutat, Alaska for 1991-2004. Data from USGS streamflow database for Alaska
(http://waterdata.usgs.gov/ak/nwis/sw).

Little work has been done to characterize the hydro-geomorphic parameters of streams and
rivers in coastal WRST. Jones and Glass (1993) measured channel characteristics and
evaluated flood potential in the glacierized upper Chitina basin in the interior region of
WRST, however no similar research has been done in the coastal region. Fluvial systems
dominated by glaciers tend to be extremely dynamic and are characterized by braided
channels resulting from the transport large loads of suspended sediment and bedload
material. These braided channels experience frequent shifts in stream geometry. Glacial
rivers within WRST have been shown to have particularly high suspended sediment loads,
which can exceed 2000 mg/L during periods of high flow (NPS 1990). In addition, channel
morphology in glacial environments is regularly affected by extreme events such as sediment
loading from landslides and outburst floods from glacier-dammed lakes (Weeks 2003).

A2c. Water resources
The land area of WRST contains one of the largest freshwater reserves in the northern
hemisphere in the form of glaciers and permanent snowfields (Weeks 2003). Freshwater
resources within the coastal region of the park include: rivers and streams, lakes and ponds,
snow and glaciers, wetlands and frost (which includes seasonal ground ice and permafrost).

A2c1. Rivers and Streams
The coastal portion of WRST contains numerous streams that flow directly into
Disenchantment Bay, Yakutat Bay, and the Gulf of Alaska. Many of the streams along the
WRST coastline are cataloged in the Yakataga Area Plan (ADNR 1995).

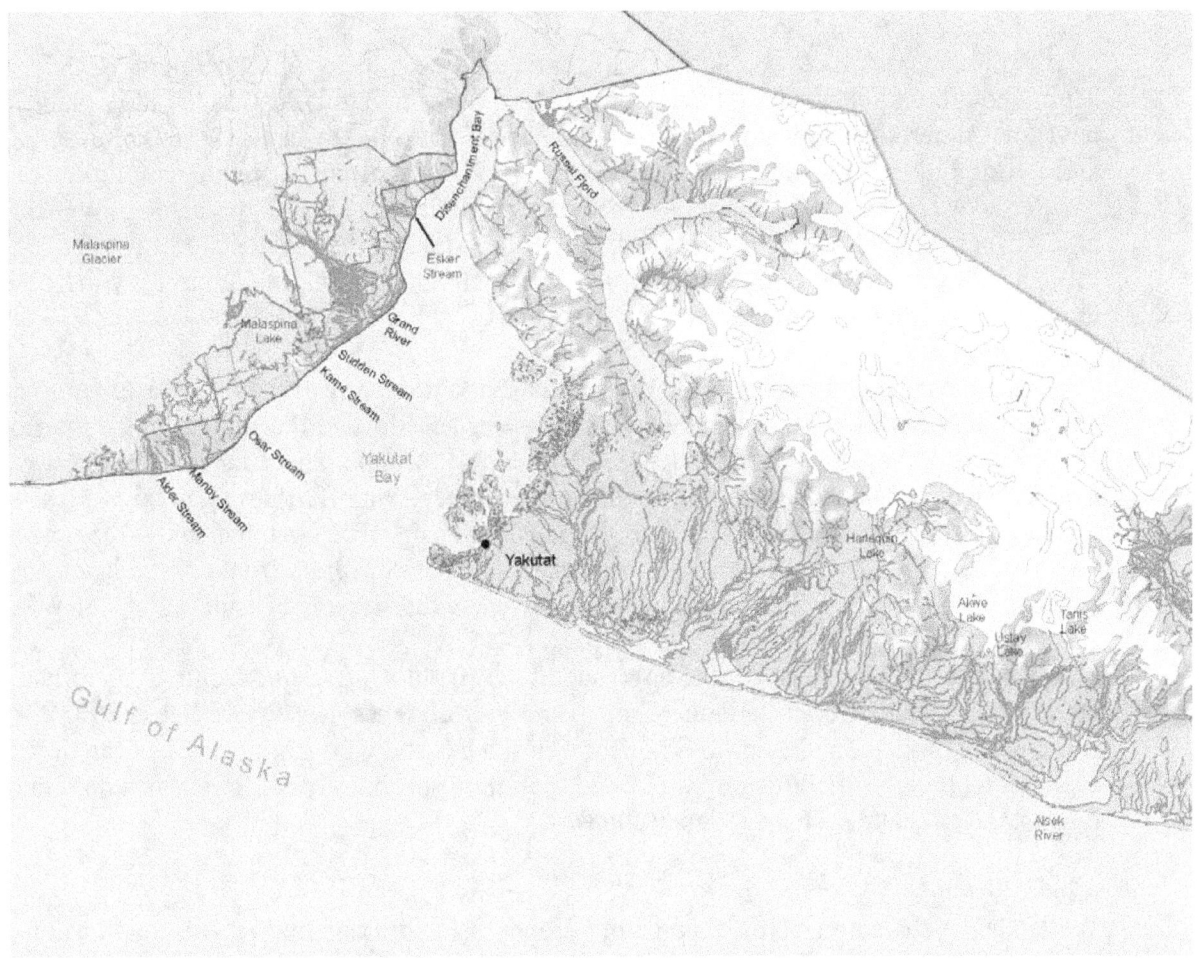

Figure 5. Lakes and streams in and around Yakutat Bay

Icy Bay, at the west end of the Park's coastline, contains a number of glacial watersheds, including Independence Creek and other numerous streams flowing from the Guyot Glacier. The Karr Hills area along the northeast portion of Icy Bay contains many streams flowing into Taan Fjord, and at the head of Icy Bay, recent glacial retreat over bedrock has created many waterfalls. The Malaspina Glacier drains into several braided rivers that flow into the Gulf of Alaska, and east of the Sitkagi Bluffs flowing from the Malaspina Glacier are Alder Stream and Manby Stream (Figure 5). Osar Stream is found near the southwest side of Malaspina Lake. Kame Stream and Sudden Stream lie near the east side of the lake and flow into Yakutat Bay. Both the Grand River and Esker Stream are contained in the Preserve and flow into Disenchantment Bay (Figure 5).

The numerous rivers and streams fed by glacial meltwater in coastal WRST have turbid waters and are typified by high gradients, large sediment loads, low levels of biotic productivity and small resident fish populations. The less abundant clearwater streams are characterized by relatively low suspended sediment loads and higher biological productivity and consequently are important as habitat for spawning fish.

13

A2c2. Lakes and Ponds

There are numerous lakes and ponds at lower elevations in the coastal region of WRST. Throughout the forelands within and immediately surrounding the park, retreating glaciers have left numerous freshwater lakes including Tanis, Ustay, Akwe, Harlequin, Malaspina and Bering Lakes (Mills and Firman 1986; Figure 5). In addition, there are a multitude of smaller lakes, many of which are unnamed, that were formed by glacial gouging (Weeks 2003). In general, biological activity and fish populations in these lakes are heavily influenced by the relative contribution of glacial meltwater because lake turbidity increases dramatically with inputs of glacial silt (NPS 1990).

There have been no limnological surveys in coastal WRST, however the physical, biological, and chemical characteristics of three lakes (Copper, Tanada, and Ptarmigan) in the interior of WRST were surveyed in the early 1990's (NPS 1994). Copper and Tanada lakes in the Copper River watershed are heavily influenced by glacial runoff. Ptarmigan lake is less glacially-influenced and drains into the White River basin. The chemical and biological characteristics of these interior lakes are likely to be quite different from coastal lakes because of the dramatic difference in climate between interior and coastal regions of WRST.

Southcentral and Southeast Alaska have one of the world's highest concentrations of lakes formed by glacial ice dams, and there are over 100 such lakes in WRST (Weeks 2003). Research in on Lemon Glacier in Southeast Alaska has shown that glacial lakes can drain rapidly and that the resulting outburst floods can transport massive volumes of sediment to downstream aquatic systems (Walter 2003).

A2c3. Wetlands

Wetlands are characterized by abundant hydrophytes, undrained hydric soils, and/or non-soil substrates that are periodically saturated or covered with water. The lower elevations in coastal WRST contain abundant wetlands. According to the US Fish and Wildlife Service National Wetlands Inventory (NWI) wetlands classification system, the wetland types in this region of the park include: estuarine and marine wetlands, freshwater emergent wetlands, freshwater forested/shrub wetlands, freshwater ponds, lakes, and riverine wetlands (USFWS 2003). Within the coastal region of the park, 75,575 acres (30,584 hectares) of wetlands have been mapped (Figure 6), the majority of these wetlands are palustrine and lacustrine. However, wetland areas have not been mapped for the northwestern portion of Yakutat Bay within the WRST boundaries (Figure 7). These wetland areas are important because they serve as an interface between terrestrial habitats and aquatic environments such as streams, lakes and near-shore marine zones. It is likely that the total area of wetlands within WRST will increase as new lands become exposed as a result of glacial recession and land surface uplift. The Alaska Department of Environmental Conservation recently developed a guidebook and methodology for functional assessment of streamside wetlands in southeastern and southcentral Alaska (Powell et al 2003). The Hydrogeomorphic Approach Methodology (HGM) provides a basis for assessing the hydrologic, biogeochemical, community (plant and faunal) support, and habitat functions of wetlands.

A2c5. Snow, Ice, and Glaciers

The coastal mountain ranges in Southcentral and Southeast Alaska contain approximately 4 million acres (1,618,742 hectares) of ice, and glacial ice is the dominant landform in the coastal region of WRST. Glaciers have profound effects on the landscape, including erosion and deposition that produce moraines, pro-glacial lakes, and eskers. Meltwater flowing from glaciers can create broad outwash zones and braided stream channels and has a dramatic influence on the annual hydrograph of glacial rivers and streams.

Glacial ice is formed when snowfall in the accumulation zone of a glacier is progressively compressed by weight of successive annual snowfalls. Glacial ice has an approximate density of 900 kg/m^3 (lighter than that of liquid water) and is characterized by air bubbles that are isolated from gas exchange with the overlying atmosphere. The mass of water contained within an individual glacier as ice and snow changes yearly depending on the glacier mass balance. The mass balance is the difference between the amount of water the glacier gains annually through snowfall and the refreezing of rainwater and the amount of water that it loses through ice melt, iceberg calving, and evaporation and sublimation. As a result, glacial mass balance is affected by shifts in local and regional temperature and precipitation regimes.

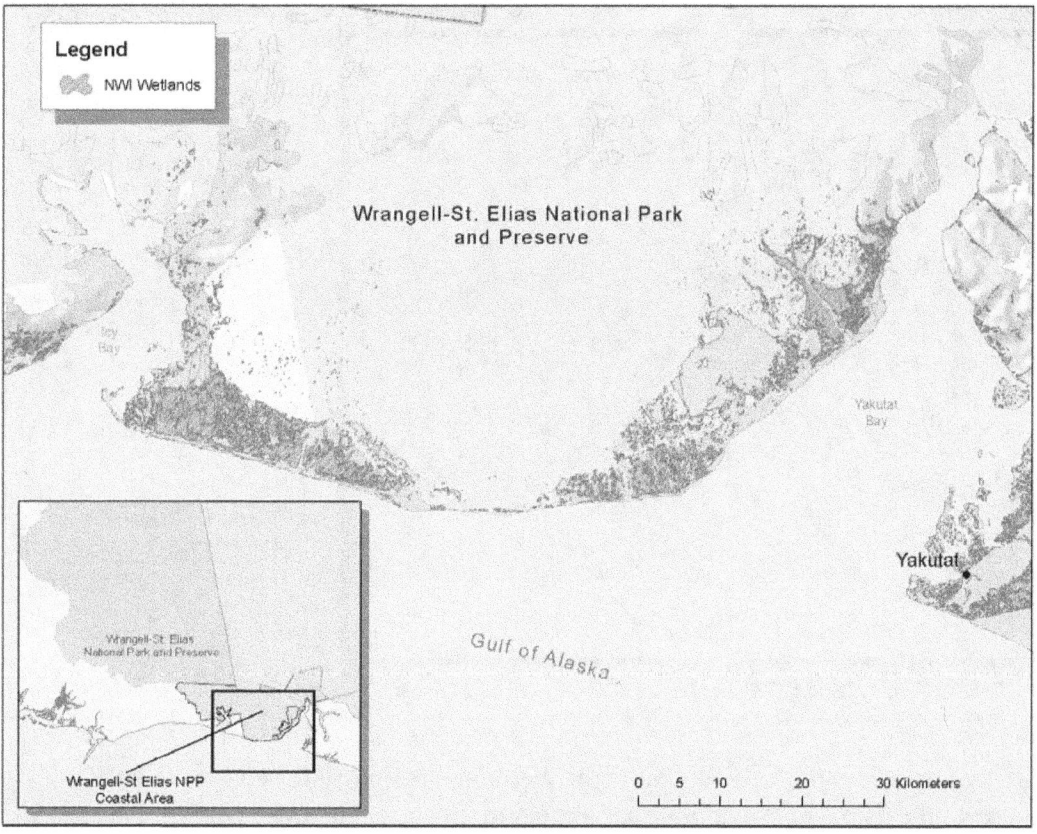

Figure 6. Wetland areas in and around the coastal region of WRST
as delineated by the USFWS National Wetland Inventory (USFWS 2003).

15

Recent studies have shown that the majority of mountain glaciers in the world have been retreating and thinning for the last several decades (e.g. Dyurgerov and Meier 2000). There are no glaciers in WRST that have ongoing programs to measure mass balance. However, several recent campaigns have looked at the volume changes on the Malaspina Glacier. Using the digital elevation models produced from Shuttle Radar Topography Mission to compare to US Geological Aerial Survey maps from 1972/3, Muskett et al (2003) estimate that for the glaciers of the Malaspina complex, mean ice thinning was 47 ± 5 m (154 ± 16 ft) for the period 1972 to 2000. This ice loss equates to approximately 60 km^3 of fresh water. More recent measurements suggest that between 2000 and 2004, ice elevation changes of -10 to -30 meters (33 to 98 ft) occurred across the central Malaspina piedmont lobe suggesting that rates of ice loss may be increasing (Sauber et al 2005). The closest glaciers to WRST that have long-term records of mass balance are the Wolverine Glacier on the Kenai Peninsula and the Gulkana Glacier in the Alaska Range, both of which are US Geological

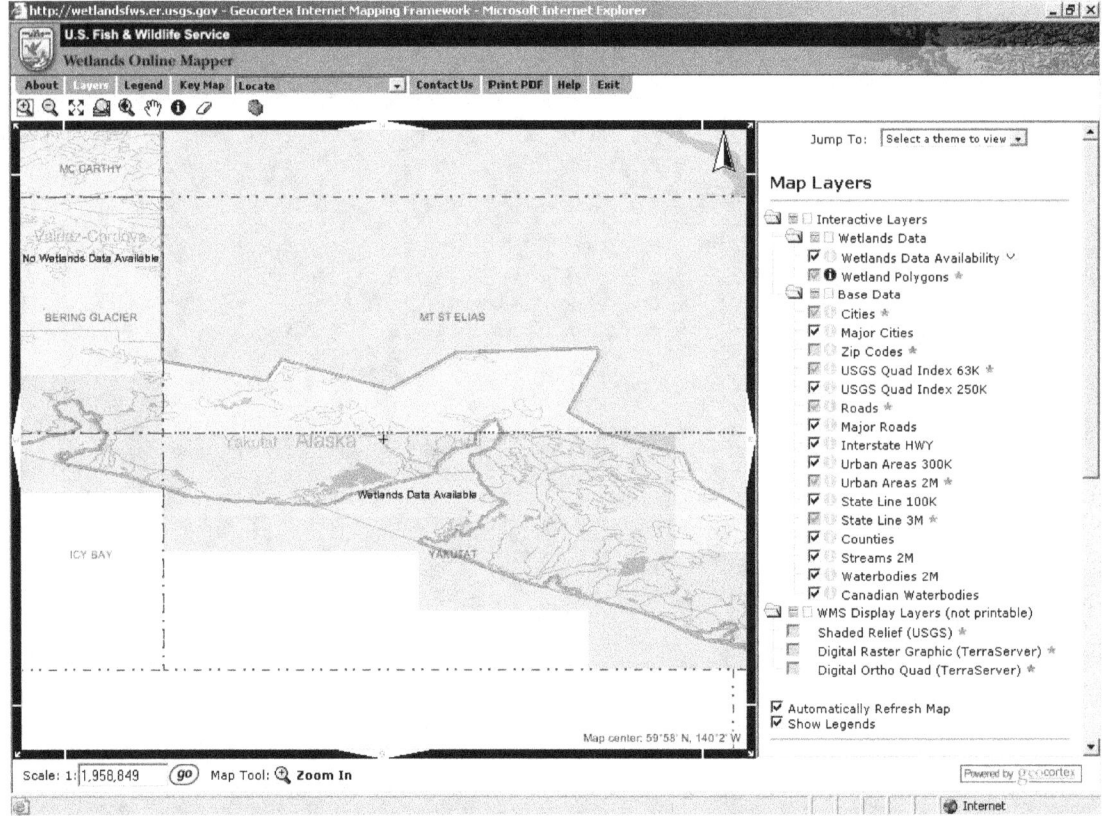

Figure 7. Coverage from the USFWS National Wetlands Inventory for coastal WRST Areas where wetlands data are available are shown in green, while areas without data are shown in tan. The upper Disenchantment Bay region within coastal WRST has not been mapped. From USFWS Online Wetlands Mapper (http://wetlandsfws.er.usgs.gov/wtlnds/launch.html).

Survey Benchmark Glaciers (http://ak.water.usgs.gov/glaciology/), and the Lemon Glacier near Juneau, which is monitored by the Juneau Icefield Research Program. The Mendenhall Glacier near Juneau also has mass balance program with measurements going back to 1998 (Motkya et al 2002).

The hydrologic system of a glacier determines the rate at which the glacier transmits and discharges freshwater. In addition, glacial hydrology can control the occurrence of outburst floods and rates of glacier sliding and surging, both of which are enhanced by the presence of meltwater at the glacier base. The hydrology of glaciers is relatively complex and not well understood. Meltwater channels can develop on the glacier surface (supraglacial), beneath the glacier (subglacial), as well as within the glacier (englacial). Recent research suggests that the hydrologic system of temperate glaciers like those found in WRST is dominated by networks of fractures within the glacier ice that convey water at relatively slow speeds (Fountain et al 2005). These fractures are regenerated seasonally and are the primary conduit through which water moves from the surface of a glacier to the glacier bed.

A2c6. Groundwater

There have been no studies on the groundwater resources in the coastal region of WRST because groundwater is not being actively withdrawn in this area of the park. Generally, groundwater within WRST is found primarily in areas characterized by unconsolidated sand, gravel, silt, and clay (Weeks 2003). Groundwater is most abundant in low-lying areas along stream courses. Wells in the park interior typically produce water from alluvial aquifers at a depth of less than forty feet (12 meters) (NPS 1990). Glacial deposits tend to be conduits for groundwater flow because of their young age and unconsolidated nature. Moreover, the outwash plains and terraces that form in front of glaciers typically contain productive aquifers (Back et al. 1988). At the terrestrial/marine interface WRST also contains coastal aquifers that are influenced by saltwater. Overall, the highly variable hydrogeologic landscape within WRST results in great variability in groundwater flow, depth, quantity, and chemistry over relatively short distances (Weeks 2003).

A2c7. Marine waters

The outer coast of WRST borders the Gulf of Alaska (GOA). The GOA is bordered by the Alaska Peninsula to the northwest and the Canadian mainland at Queen Charlotte Sound to the southeast (Figure 8). Dominant habitats include continental shelf, slope and abyssal plain. Within the GOA, the continental shelf area represents more then 12 % of the continental shelf holdings of the US (Hood 1986). The width of the continental shelf ranges from 5 km in the southeast to nearly 200 km around Kodiak Island (Weingartner et al. 2005). Abyssal depths (>7000 m) occur in the northwest portion of the GOA within the Aleutian Trench. Slope and plain environments are dotted with subsurface banks, ridges, and seamounts which rise from over a kilometer depth to within a few hundred meters of the surface. Fjords, convoluted shorelines, underwater canyons and ridges, and multiple islands create a mosaic of geological features that contribute to a complex oceanographic domain. The oceanography of the GOA is composed of gyres, surface currents, predominant downwellings, and punctuated localized upwellings. Offshore circulation is dominated by a cyclonic subarctic gyre. The sluggish, easterly-flowing North Pacific Current bifurcates near

52° N and becomes the Alaska Current (AC) northward (Figure 8) and the California Current southward. The Alaska Coastal Current (ACC), inshore of the AC, is a low-salinity, cyclonic (counter-clockwise), fast-moving (13 – 133 cm/s) current driven by winds and density gradients established through freshwater input (Hood 1986). Precipitation within the GOA ranges from 2 – 6 m per annum (Weingartner et al. 2005). The region is affected by intense winter storms that frequently become trapped or stalled by the surrounding rugged coastal topography (Wilson & Overland 1986, Royer 1998). Persistent cyclonic winds, coupled with onshore surface Ekman transport promote downwelling favorable conditions for much of the GOA, however episodic and local upwelling may be generated by eddies or other local geography. Despite predominant downwelling, the Gulf of Alaska is a productive ecosystem. Nutrients are supplied from small-scale upwelling, eddies, shear, Ekman transport, resuspension of shelf sediments and river discharge (Stabeno et al. 2004). Eddies are frequently generated off the British Columbia coast (Crawford et al. 2002) and in Southeast Alaska near Sikta and propagate through the GOA along the ACC. Eddies in the GOA range from 10-50 km and normally persist for 1 to 4 weeks (Bograd et al. 1994). The arrival of eddies to the shore may increase larval recruitment via entrainment of fish and shellfish larvae within water conditions favorable to survival (Incze et al. 1989, Schumacher et al. 1993), whereas the generation of eddies may decrease larval recruitment via advection (Sinclair & Crawford 2005).

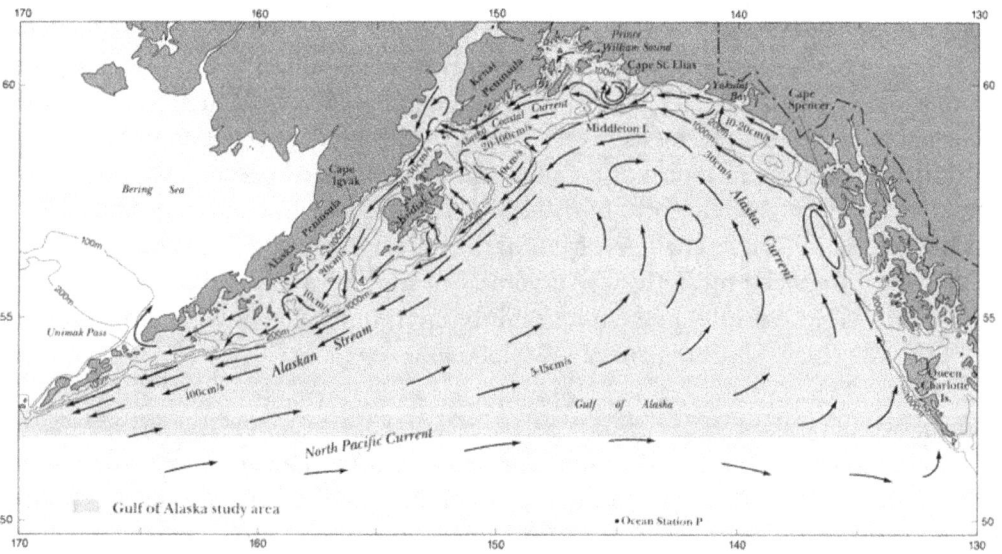

Figure 8. Predominant currents in the GOA (Reed & Schumacher 1986).

The GOA is meteorologically active and dominated by a persistently-located area of low pressure known as the Aleutian Low (Mundy & Olsson 2005). Winter storms, characterized by low sea-level pressures, can routinely produce >15 m waves and gale strength winds (Wilson & Overland 1986). The Low oscillates in strength and location throughout the year but maintains its influence on the regional climate (Wilson & Overland 1986, Mundy & Olsson 2005). The Pacific Decadal Oscillation (PDO) and the El Niño Southern Oscillation (ENSO) are global-scale atmospheric and oceanic conditions that influence climate, weather events, circulation, and ultimately, the biology of the GOA. The PDO is characterized by descriptive weather indices that track anomalies of sea surface temperature, wind stress, and sea level atmospheric pressure (Hare et al. 1999). Wintertime location of the Aleutian Low creates a proxy for which regime the PDO is characterized. A negative PDO occurs when the Aleutian Low is centered in the southwestern GOA, over the Aleutians and southern Bering Sea. A positive PDO occurs when the Aleutian Low has a northeastern GOA locus, and the climate of the GOA is characterized by warmer sea surface temperatures, higher precipitation, and windier conditions (Hare et al. 1999). Opposite patterns for the Gulf are observed during negative phases of the PDO. Winters with strong Aleutian Lows tend to be associated with ENSO warming events (Niebauer 1988). During a warming event (El Niño), sea levels rise, upwelling shuts off, and water temperatures in equatorial Pacific near Peru may rise as much as 5.4° C. During a cool phase (La Niña), cooler surface waters (< 20° C) extend offshore of Peru and intensify upwelling currents in that region. Warming in the equatorial Pacific is not always associated with intensification of the Aleutian Low and vice-versa.

Water quality in marine waters was recently surveyed by the Environmental Monitoring and Assessment Program (EMAP), which sampled throughout Southeast Alaska (Figure 9) in 2004 including two stations in Yakutat Bay and one site in Icy Bay. At 40 stations, physical properties (conductivity, temperature, salinity, pH, dissolved oxygen, chlorophyll fluorescence), water (nutrients, chlorophyll a, and total suspended solids), sediment (contaminants, infauna), and benthic fish and invertebrates (trawl) were sampled. At 11 additional stations, water was sampled for bacteria as a part of the ADEC cruise ship program. Data from this sampling effort was not available at the time of publication of this report. The final report for Southeast EMAP is expected to be released in 2007 from ADEC.

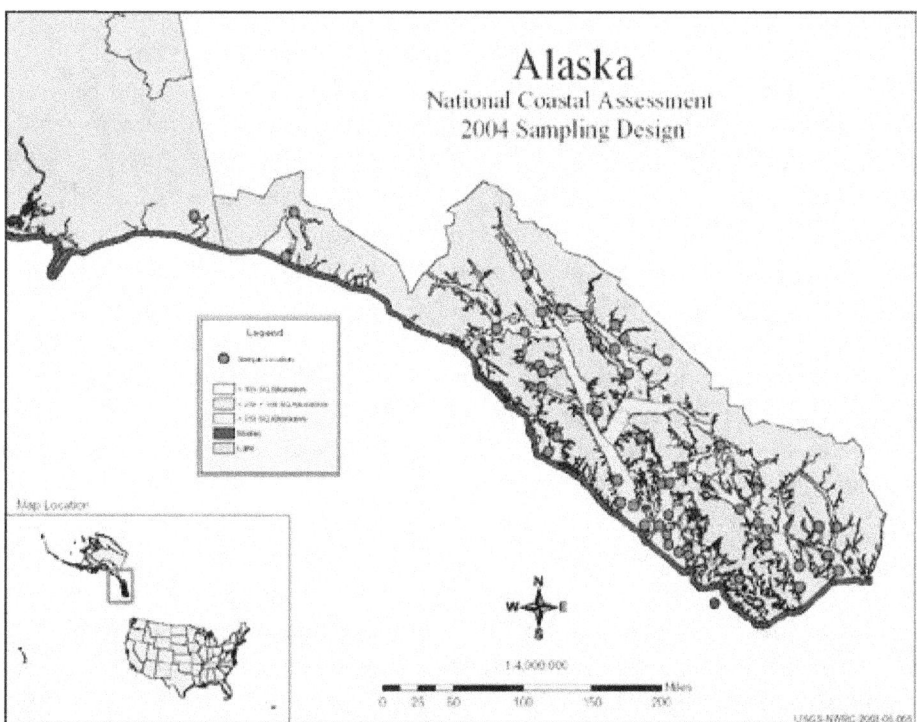

Figure 9. Sites sampled by EMAP in Southeast Alaska in 2004
From http://www.dec.state.ak.us/water/wqamp/emap_se.htm

A3. Biological resources

A3a. Marine

The southern boundary of the coastal region of WRST consists of 125 miles (201 km) of coastline along the Gulf of Alaska (Weeks 2003), including the Malaspina Forelands adjacent to the Malaspina Glacier, and portions of Icy Bay, Yakutat Bay, and Disenchantment Bay. Several surveys of birds and marine mammals have been completed for coastal WRST, along the Malaspina Forelands, Yakutat Bay, Disenchantment Bay and the Yakutat Forelands (Patten 1981, Kozie 1993, Kozie et al 1996, Andres and Browne 1998).

Harbor seals (*Phoca vitulina*) inhabit the WRST coast (Kozie 1993) and are species of concern because of declines in their populations in Alaska. In Glacier Bay, populations have declined as much as 70% in the most recent decade (Mathews and Kelly 1996, Mathews and Pendleton 2000). Traditional knowledge indicates that harbor seals in WRST are declining (personal communication, Beth Mathews, Assistant Professor of Biology, University of Alaska Southeast, 2005), however limited data precludes quantitative documentation of a decline. Harbor seals use the WRST coastline as breeding and feeding grounds. Icebergs provide important habitat for harbor seal pupping and molting from May to July and molting from June to October (ADNR 1995). Harbor seal pupping and subsistence seal harvesting occurs in Disenchantment Bay and in upper and eastern Icy Bay, and harbor seals are concentrated at Sudden Stream (ADNR 1995). Future studies will examine predation on harbor seals in Disenchantment Bay (personal communication, Beth Mathews, Assistant Professor of Biology, University of Alaska Southeast, 2005).

Steller sea lions (*Eumetopias jubatus*) are federally listed as endangered west of Cape Suckling due to declining populations throughout the western Gulf of Alaska and Bering Sea regions (Sease and Loughlin 1997, Gelatt et al. 2004), however the eastern stock in Southeast Alaska is stable but considered threatened (Calkins et al. 1999, Gelatt et al. 2004). The NPS did not find any Steller sea lions in WRST coastal areas during aerial surveys in 2003 and 2004, however the available habitat is very limited (personal communication, Mason Reid, Wildlife Biologist, Wrangell – St. Elias National Park and Preserve, 2005). Current sea otter distributions are discontinuous in the WRST coastal areas and are still recovering from commercial harvesting in the mid-1700s through 1800s. USFWS aerial surveys in 1995 and 1996 yielded an overall sea otter population estimate of 404 for Yakutat Bay, including Disenchantment Bay, Russell Fjord and Nunatak Fjord (Doroff and Gorbics 1998). Sea otters were not observed during the surveys along the outer coast from Kaliakh River to Point Manby nor in Icy Bay (Doroff and Gorbics 1998).

Other marine mammals that have been observed in WRST include harbor porpoise (*Phocoena phocoena*) in Icy Bay and Malasapina Forelands, humpback whale (*Megaptera novaeangliae*), in Malaspina Forelands (Kozie 1993), orca (*Orcinus orca*) and Dall porpoises (*Phocoena dalli*) (NPS 2005). Beluga whales (*Delphinapterus leucas*) have been seen in the Grand Wash Slough along the Malaspina Forelands (NPS 1986) and in Yakutat and Disenchantment Bay (Hubbard et al. 1999).

Many birds inhabit the WRST coastal area (see Appendix A for species list). Seabird surveys along the Malaspina Forelands were dominated by Kittlitz's (*Brachyramphus brevirostris*) and marbled murrelets (*Brachyramphus marmoratus*) and glaucous-winged gulls (*Larus glaucescens*) (Kozie 1993). Also found in WRSTs coastal area are trumpeter swans (*Olor buccinator*), bald eagles (*Haliaeetus leucocephalus*), and golden eagles (*Aquila chrysaetos*) (Weeks 2003). Bald eagles (*Haliaeetus leucocephalus*) are known to nest along the Malaspina Forelands (Kozie 1993). In Icy Bay, several colonies of Arctic (*Sterna paradisaea*) and Aleutian terns (*Sterna aleutica*) nest on Riou Spit, glaucous-winged gulls nest in a large colony on Gull Island, and a few other species, including black oystercatchers (*Haematopus bachmani*), nest in smaller numbers in both of these locations (Kozie et al. 1996). Along with the Malaspina Forelands and Icy Bay, estuaries in Russell fjord, the Sitkagi Bluffs, and the Yakutat Forelands are considered extremely important due to their productivity and maintenance of high avian biomass (Patten 1981).

Limited sampling of fishes in 2001-2002 in Icy and Yakutat Bays within 5.6 km (3.5 miles) of the shore was completed using bottom trawls, herring trawls, and beach seining, although floating ice restricted areas that could be sampled (Arimitsu et al. 2003). This sampling captured 31 fish species in Icy and Yakutat Bays, 16 species in pelagic habitats (herring trawls), 14 species in demersal habitats (bottom trawls), and 14 species in nearshore habitats (beach seines) (Table 1, Armitsu et al. 2003). Sampling was limited and only conducted during summer months, and therefore additional species may be found during increased sampling and at other times of the year. Armitsu et al. (2003) recommend pelagic, demersal, and nearshore sampling during winter, fall, and spring seasons.

A3b. Intertidal

WRST has over 1,000 acres (405 hectares) of diverse intertidal communities, however very little is known about the intertidal flora and fauna and no surveys or monitoring have been conducted (personal communication, Lewis Sharman, Ecologist, Glacier Bay National Park and Preserve, 2005). Intertidal regions along coastal WRST are exposed to severe storms. Extremely large waves are driven onto outer beaches when winds reach velocities greater than 160 kph (99 mph), which inundates large estuarine areas with saltwater and causes substantial disturbance (Patten 1981).

The coast of WRST provides important habitat for spawning eulachon (*Thaleichthys pacificus*), an anadromous smelt that spawns in dense concentrations in coastal freshwater streams in the spring. Aggregations of eulachon during spawning provide food for predatory fish, marine mammals, and marine birds and, as such, plays an important part in nearshore marine ecological cycles (Patten 1981). Once eulachon larvae hatch, they drift downstream and into intertidal areas, nearshore sounds, straits, and fjords, and the sea (Patten 1981).

ShoreZone is a project sponsored by multiple agencies and organizations that conducted aerial surveys of intertidal regions in Southeast Alaska in 2004-2005. This project aerially surveyed intertidal and shallow subtidal areas to identify shoreline morphology, substrate, wave exposure, and biota of intertidal and nearshore habitats. This coastal habitat mapping effort produced an online database with interactive GIS layers, digital maps, aerial images and video (http://mapping.fakr.noaa.gov/Website/ShoreZone/). In 2005, ShoreZone surveyed Icy Bay and Yakutat Bay (including Russell Fjord) and future plans are to cover all of Southeast Alaska. At the time of publication of this report, ShoreZone data layers, video, and photos were not yet available, but should become available in 2006.

Table 1. Fishes collected during fish inventory surveys in 2001-2002 (Armitsu et al. 2003). H = caught in herring trawl. B = caught in bottom trawl. S = caught in beach seine.

Clupeidae	*Clupea pallasii*	Pacific herring	H, S
Osmeridae	*Mallotus villosus*	capelin	H, B, S
Osmeridae	*Spirinchus thaleichthys*	longfin smelt	H
Osmeridae	*Hypomesus pretiosus*	surf smelt	S
Osmeridae	*Thaleichthys pacificus*	eulachon	H
Salmonidae	*Oncorhynchus gorbuscha*	pink salmon	H, S
Gadidae	*Gadus macrocephalus*	Pacific cod	H
Gadidae	*Theragra chalcogramma*	walleye pollock	H, B
Hexagrammidae	*Hexagrammos lagocephalus*	rock greenling	S
Hexagrammidae	*Hexagrammos stelleri*	whitespotted greenling	S
Hemitripteridae	*Hemitripterus bolini*	bigmouth sculpin	B
Psychrolutidae	*Dasycottus setiger*	spineyhead sculpin	B
Psychrolutidae	*Psychrolutes sigalutes*	soft sculpin	H
Cottidae	*Enophrys bison*	buffalo sculpin	S
Cottidae	*Myoxocephalus polyacanthochephalus*	great sculpin	S
Cottidae	*Oligocottus maculosus*	tidepool sculpin	S
Cyclopteridae	*Eumicrotremus orbis*	Pacific spiny lumpsucker	H, B
Zoarcidae	*Lycodes palearis*	wattled eelpout	H, B
Zoarcidae	*Lycodes brevipes*	shortfin eelpout	B
Stichaeidae	*Lumpenella longirostris*	longsnout prickleback	B
Stichaeidae	*Lumpenus sagitta*	snake prickleback	H, B, S
Stichaeidae	*Lumpenus maculatus*	daubed shanny	H, B
Stichaeidae	*Anisarchus medius*	stout eelblenny	H, B
Trichodontidae	*Trichodon trichodon*	Pacific sandfish	H, S
Pholidae	*Pholis laeta*	crescent gunnel	S
Ammodytidae	*Ammodytes hexapterus*	Pacific sand lance	H, S
Pleuronectidae	*Lyopsetta exilis*	slender sole	H
Pleuronectidae	*Atheresthes stomias*	arrowtooth flounder	B
Pleuronectidae	*Hippoglossoides elassodon*	flathead sole	B
Pleuronectidae	*Microstomus pacificus*	dover sole	B
Pleuronectidae	*Platichthys stellatus*	starry flounder	S

A3c. Wetlands

Wetlands in WRST are found in a variety of areas including: adjacent to streams and lakes, in wet tundra areas, shallow tundra ponds, wet shrub scrub, and forested wetlands (Weeks 2003). Along the coastline, wetlands are found in lower elevation areas along the mouth of coastal streams. Biological communities in WRST wetlands are dominated by sedges (*Carex aquatilis, C. canescens, C. limosa, C. saxatilis, C. utriculata*, and several species of *Eriophorum* [including *E. angustifolium, E. russoleum* and *E. vaginatum*]), mosses, grasses (*Arctagrostis latifolia, Arctophila fulva* and *Calamagrostis Canadensis*), forbs and scattered shrubs (Cassandra [*Chamaedaphne calyculata*], sweetgale [*Myrica gale*] and Bog rosemary [*Andromeda polifolia*]) (NPS 2005). Horsetails (*Equisetum palustre* and *E. fluviatile*), spike rush (*Eleocharis palustris*), and buckbean (*Menyanthes trifoliata*) are also common and widespread in lowland wetlands (NPS 2005).

Cook (1990a) sampled vegetation at the Icy Bay Mine Site located on Independence Creek in west Icy Bay on the border of WRST (Figure 10). This survey documented 11 obligate wetland species which almost always occur under natural conditions in wetlands (Reed 1988), and 10 facultative wetland species which usually occurs in wetlands, but occasionally are found in nonwetlands (Cook 1990a). The complete plant list, showing the status of wetland plants, can be found in Appendix B. The NPS (1990) also did a vegetative survey at the east Sitkagi Bluffs area along the Malaspina forelands. This survey documented four species of plants associated with wetlands. A complete species list for the east Sitkagi Bluffs is found in Appendix C.

A3d. Uplands

The forest composition of WRST lowlands ranges from coastal Sitka spruce and western hemlock forests along the Malaspina Forelands to taiga forests of the interior. Lowland basins and north-facing slopes that blanket areas of permafrost support slow-growing black spruce (*Picea mariana*) and muskeg (NPS 2005). The most common understory shrubs in these areas include Alder (*Alnus crispa*), Dwarf birch (*Betula glandulosa*), Crowberry (*Empetrum nigrum*), Labrador tea (*Ledum groenlandicum*), Shrub cinquefoil (*Potentilla fruticosa*), several willows (including *Salix alaxensis, S. arbusculoides, S. glauca,* and *S. planifolia ssp. pulchra*) and blueberry (*Vaccinium uliginosum*) (NPS 2005). Dense stands of willows thrive along the streambanks of WRST (NPS 1986). River mosses common to the lowlands include *Hylocomium splendens, Pleurozium schreberi* and *Sphagnum spp.* (NPS 2005).

The uplands of WRST have better drainage and thus have different flora than the lowlands and areas underlain by permafrost. Thickets of alder (*Alnus crispa*) and willow (*Salix spp*) line major rivers, while colonial herbs grow in newly abandoned channels (NPS 2005). White spruce (Picea glauca) occurs along river bottoms (Weeks 2003). White spruce forests are also occasionally mixed with paper birch (*Betula resinifera*) in the upland hillsides of the Park. Aspen (*Populus tremuloides*) is found in dry or recently burned sites (NPS 2005). On south-facing slopes, spruce forests are replaced by aspen woodland as the slope increases (NPS 2005). The driest sites in the WRST forest zone have dry steppe vegetation dominated by grasses, sagebrush, scattered shrubs of juniper and a variety of herbaceous perennials (NPS 2005). Upland dry site plant communities harbor a comparatively large numbers of rare plant species. Plant communities of the southern part of WRST include *Elymus calderi* and *Juniperus horizontalis*, but are absent from northern locations (NPS 2005).

Patten (1981) reports that the forests along the Malaspina Forelands are dominated by black cottonwood (*Populus trichocarpa*) along with the occasional spruce. Riparian areas in the forelands are typically a mosaic of willow, alder, cottonwood, and spruce. Upland along the Grand Wash are slightly elevated areas of herbaceous meadows, black cottonwood, willow, and alder (Patten 1981). Sudden Stream has two branches which drain Malaspina Lake, and these are bordered by dense willow, cottonwood, and scattered spruce (Patten 1981). Cook (1988) reports that midgrass herb vegetation grows along the banks of Sudden Stream, and certain areas along Sudden Stream are dominated by alder and willow. An open black cottonwood forest grows continuously from Sudden Stream southwest to Kame Stream and northwest to Malaspina Lake, and this was found to be interspersed with alder scrub throughout the area. Patten (1981) reports that the land north and west of Point Manby is dominated by spruce forest. The spruce forest ends abruptly at Manby Stream, and muskeg dominates further west of this area. The Sitkagi Bluffs are composed of alder, spruce, and cottonwood (Patten 1981). The forest adjacent to the East Sitkagi Bluffs is a mix of black cottonwood and sitka spruce with a well developed understory (NPS 1990). NPS (1990) gives a list of all species observed in the east Sitkagi Bluffs from a brief survey, which include four shrub, eighteen forb, five graminoid, three lower vascular and nine non-vascular taxa. A complete plant species list for the Sitkagi Bluffs is found in Appendix C (NPS 1990). In a survey done at Independence Creek along west Icy Bay, Cook (1990a) reports that the forest upland of the creek is composed of Sitka spruce and black cottonwood. A complete plant species list for the Icy Bay Mine Site is found in Appendix B (Cook 1990a). The vegetation of West Icy Bay has also been monitored for a study on glacial succession by Beck (1989). This report gives a detailed list of species and their abundance along the "Arrowhead", a triangular peninsula located on the western shore of Icy Bay. This report states that the "distal end" or upland area of the Arrowhead is comprised of an alder vegetation community. This is a tall shrub community dominated by alder with some willow (*S. alaxensis, s. sitchensis, S. commutata*), and black cottonwood.

Some of the major wildlife species found along the WRST coast include moose (*Alces alces gigas*), brown bears (*Ursus arctos horribilis*), black bears (*Ursus americanus*), wolves (*Canis lupus*), and numerous furbearers (Mills and Firman 1986, Weeks 2003). Contemporary trapping records show the presence of red fox (*Vulpes vulpes*), lynx (*Lynx canadensis*), wolverine (*Gulo gulo*), river otter (*Lontra canadensis*), beaver (*Castor canadensis*), mink (*Mustela vison*) and marten (*Martes americana*) along the coast of WRST (Mills and Firman 1986). Other game species along the coast include Dall sheep (*Ovis dalli*) and mountain goat (*Oreamnos americanus*) (Mills and Firman 1986). WRST also contains a remarkable diversity of dipertans (flies and their allies), odonata (dragonflies and their allies), a small population of wood frogs (*Rana spp*) and even salamaders (*Tariches spp*), which survive the winters by burrowing deep within the soil (NPS 2005).

A3e. Freshwater bodies

Glacial rivers and streams within coastal WRST are not highly productive due to the high magnitude of suspended silt they entrain and transport. Yet, many of these waterways typically provide migration routes for salmon reaching their spawning sites and rearing habitat in upstream clearwater tributaries and lakes (Weeks, 2003). As part of the NPS Inventory and Monitoring Program, a freshwater fish inventory was conducted in WRST (Markis et al. 2004). Species that were documented in coastal streams of WRST include chinook or king salmon (*Oncorhynchus tshawytscha*), costrange sculpin (*Cottus aleuticus*), coho or silver salmon (*Oncorhunchus kisutch*), Dolly Varden (*Salvelinus malma*), eulachon (*Thaleichthys pacificus*), slimy sculpin (*Cottus cogatus*), starry flounder (*Platichthys stellatus*), and threespine stickleback (*Gasterosteus aculeatus*). Of these fish inventoried, the coastrange sculpin, eulachon, slimy sculpin, starry flounder, and threespine stickleback were expected but previously undocumented.

Many streams along coastal WRST support anadromous fish populations, including Alder Stream, Manby Stream, Oscar Stream, Sudden Stream, the Grand Wash River, Esker Stream, and many unnamed streams in Icy Bay and other areas of coastal WRST (ADFG 2005). The Yakataga Area Plan indicates that commercial set net fishing occurs at several stream mouths on the Malaspina Forelands, including Manby Stream, Spoon River, Sudden Stream, and Esker Stream (ADNR 1995). In glacial systems where new stream systems are in the process of developing, fish habitat improves as sediment loads decline and variations in water flow stabilize. In particular, streams provide better fish habitat for spawning and rearing once pools develop, riparian cover becomes established, and sediment transport declines after deglaciation (Sidle and Milner 1989). As deglaciation continues, it is expected that additional anadromous fish habitat will be created.

The maintenance of healthy salmon stocks and appropriate fish passage through coastal streams and rivers in southeast Alaska is important not only for fisheries resources, but also because spawning salmonids have significant impacts on biological resources in terrestrial and freshwater aquatic ecosystems (Gende et al 2002). When salmon return to their natal streams to spawn, they transport marine nutrients and energy across ecosystem boundaries, and their carcasses release large quantities of "marine-derived nutrients" to freshwater and terrestrial ecosystems (Willson et al. 1998, Cederholm et al. 1999, Johnston et al. 2004). These nutrients are important to the overall health of coastal watersheds (Bryant and Everest 1998) and can greatly affect stream productivity (Wipfli et al. 1998, Chaloner and Wipfli 2002). In particular, seasonal pulses of salmon carcasses can dramatically elevate streamwater nutrients levels (Mitchell and Lambertti 2005), thereby affecting primary and secondary productivity in receiving streams. In addition, carcasses that end up in the riparian zone as a result of changes in stream discharge, scavenging, or bear activity provide a substantial input of nutrients such as nitrogen and phosphorus to riparian soils (Gende et al in prep). These nutrients can be rapidly assimilated by microbial communities and vegetation in the riparian environment (Bilby et al 1996) and have been hypothesized to increase the growth rate of trees in the riparian forest (Helfield and Naiman 2001). These findings highlight the ecological importance of salmon in coastal ecosystems and suggest that fisheries management decisions related to salmon have the potential to affect terrestrial biological resources within WRST.

B. Water Resources Assessment

B1. Water quality

Water quality in coastal watersheds and coastal areas of WRST is not monitored. Due to the remote location and low level of human activity, it is assumed that water quality within the coastal areas of WRST is in good condition. Unlike northern and central areas of WRST, coastal watersheds have been subject to little mineral exploration and development. The only source of information on the water quality of coastal rivers and streams within WRST is a 1989 NPS field survey on the environmental impacts of a sand and gravel mining operation near the mouth of Independence Creek, immediately south of the WRST boundary and approximately 100 m (328 ft) from the high tide line in Icy Bay (Figure 10; Cook 1990a). WRST staff collected information on water temperature, conductivity, pH, dissolved oxygen, hardness, arsenic, lead, iron, total suspended solids and discharge in the drainage slough behind the camp and 60m (197 ft) from the mouth of Independence Creek. Measured iron concentration was 20.5 mg/l, which is twenty times the EPA standard for freshwater aquatic life and may indicate the presence of an upstream ore deposit (Cook 1990a). Total suspended solids were also high, at 1050 mg/l, which was explained by the warm weather at the time of sampling. Melting of the Independence Glacier, from which Independence Creek originates, provides the stream with higher suspended particle loads. All other parameters measured (Table 2) were within normal ranges set by the EPA and the State of Alaska.

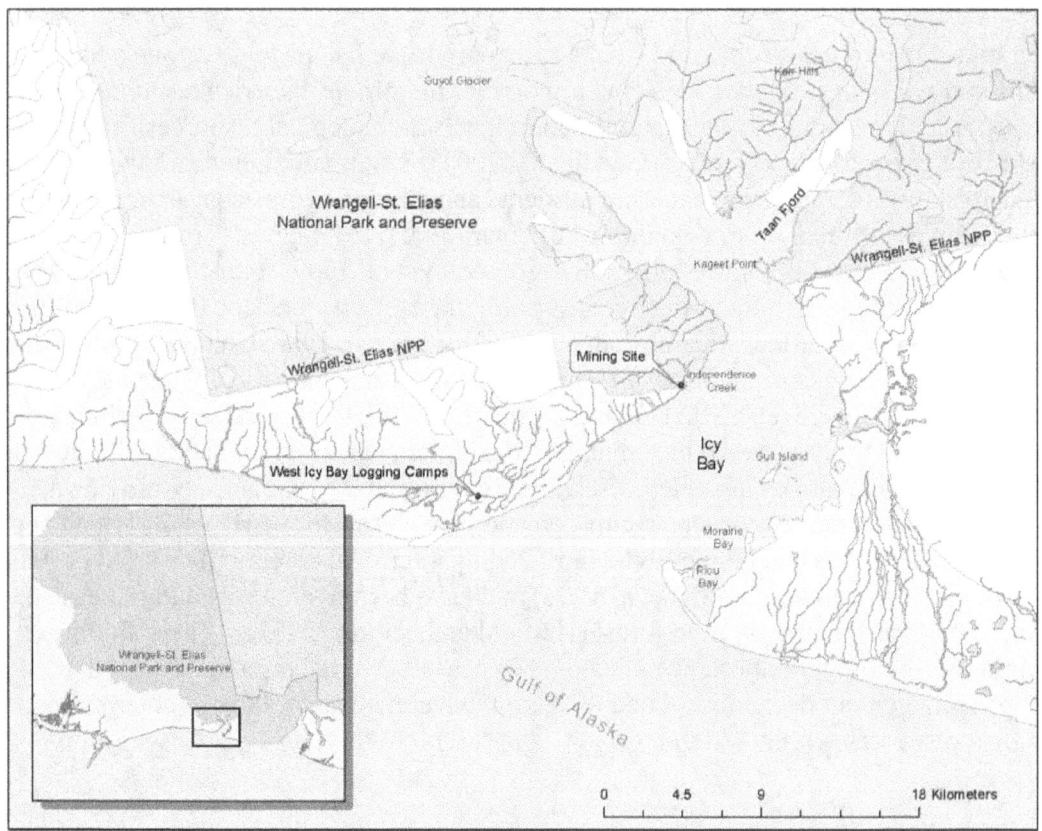

Figure 10. Location of mining site at Independence Creek and west Icy Bay logging camps.

Table 2. Water quality from two locations near Icy Bay mine site 21, August 1989
Analysis of metals and total suspended solids was done by Northern Testing Laboratory, Anchorage, Alaska, from Cook (1990a).

Site	Drainage behind mine camp	60m from mouth of Independence Creek
Water Temperature (°C)	16.0	13.0
Turbidity (NTU)	13.0	252.0
Conductivity (UMHOS)	245.0	80.0
pH	7.39	7.27
Dissolved Oxygen (mg/l)	5.0	8.0
Alkalinity (mg/l)	143.0	46.0
Hardness (mg/l)	170.0	56.0
Settleable solids (mg/l)	0.2	0.7
Width (ft.)	14.0	41.2
Depth (ft.)	0.700	0.784
Velocity (ft./s)	0.00	2.59
Discharge (CFS)	0.000	119.962
Arsenic (mg/l)	0.0060	0.025
Iron (mg/l)	0.592	20.500
Lead (mg/l)	0.0030	0.0060
Total Suspended Solids	3.4	1050.0

The main source of information summarizing water quality of rivers and streams within WRST is a water resources scoping report by Weeks (2003), however this report contains no water quality information on coastal streams; it does provide data on inland water bodies (Nabesna, Chisana, Granite Peak, Nizina, and Kennicott Rivers) (Weeks 2003). According to this report, most glacial and non-glacial streams in inland WRST had a pH near neutral (7.0). Hardness, alkalinity, and heavy metal concentrations all varied among streams due to the different lithologic compositions of the watersheds, although most streams were characterized as moderately hard (75-150 mg/L calcium carbonate). Glacial streams in the Park carried high sediment loads and were highly turbid. Non-glacial streams were characterized by low sediment and low turbidity, except during high flow conditions. Due to the constant input of glacial meltwater, water temperatures in glacial streams were near freezing throughout the summer.

Because groundwater studies have not been carried out along the coastline of WRST, specific information for this area is not available. The nearest groundwater study site is in the northern central areas of WRST (NPS 1990). The NPS study does not provide any data, but it qualitatively states that groundwater in that region of WRST has naturally high concentrations of metals, particularly iron, due to contact with highly mineralized surfaces and restriction of water circulation by permafrost (NPS 1990). Some groundwater was found in the area to be saline due to underlying marine sedimentary deposits (NPS 1990).

According to WRSTs General Park Management Plan (1986), maintenance of water quality within the Park is carried out by the NPS, the Alaska Department of Environmental Conservation (ADEC), and the Environmental Protection Agency (EPA). The ADEC and the EPA enforce both air and water quality regulations on NPS lands, and the ADEC must be consulted prior to any NPS development that may have adverse effects on water quality within the Park (NPS 1986). Water quality standards for the state of Alaska can be found on the ADEC's website http://www.dec.state.ak.us/water/wqsar/wqs/wqs.htm and are summarized in Appendix D.

Precipitation

The chemistry of precipitation is not currently being monitored in coastal WRST; however, a new National Atmospheric Deposition Program (NADP) site was established in southeastern Alaska north of Juneau in 2004. The NADP is a nationwide network contains more than 200 precipitation chemistry monitoring in the continental United States, Alaska, Puerto Rico, and the Virgin Islands. There are 4 NADP sites in Alaska, two of which are administered by the National Park Service (Denali and Gates of the Arctic). The NADP site near Juneau (NADP #AK02) is the closest station to WRST and is likely representative of precipitation received in coastal WRST. Preliminary data from the Juneau NADP site show a predominance of marine aerosols (chlorine, sulfate, and sodium) and very low levels of nitrogen (ammonium and nitrate) compared to sites in the contiguous United States (E. Hood, unpublished data). Data on precipitation chemistry in Alaska are available through the NADP website (http://nadp.sws.uiuc.edu/sites/ntnmap.asp?).

B2. Water quality impairments

B2a. Sudden Stream, Yakutat Bay

In May of 1962, the Colorado Oil and Gas Corporation (COGO) drilled two wells on Sudden Stream (Figure 11). (Malaspina Unit No. 1 and Malaspina Unit No.1-A) (Bleakley 2002). Both wells were plugged and abandoned due to a drilling problem in Unit No. 1 and the absence of oil and gas in Unit No.1-A (NPS 1992). A warehouse was constructed at this time to store drilling muds and additives, and this too was abandoned in 1962. The warehouse eventually collapsed, exposing the storage containers, and causing their contents to leak over time (ENSR Consulting and Engineering 1991).

The Sudden Stream site was confirmed to be contaminated in 1984 after soil samples were taken by WRST staff. The area was sampled more thoroughly in 1987 and 1989, resulting in the determination that the water and soil within 200 feet (61 meters) of the site contained elevated levels of barium and chromium and that tissues of fish and mollusks from the area had elevated levels of barium (NPS. n.d. 1985-1992.). Because elevated levels of chromium and barium were found in samples of soil and groundwater near the site, vegetation samples were analyzed for these contaminants in 1988. Results from this study indicated that chromium and barium concentrations were elevated in five of the seven plant species sampled (NPS n.d.1988).

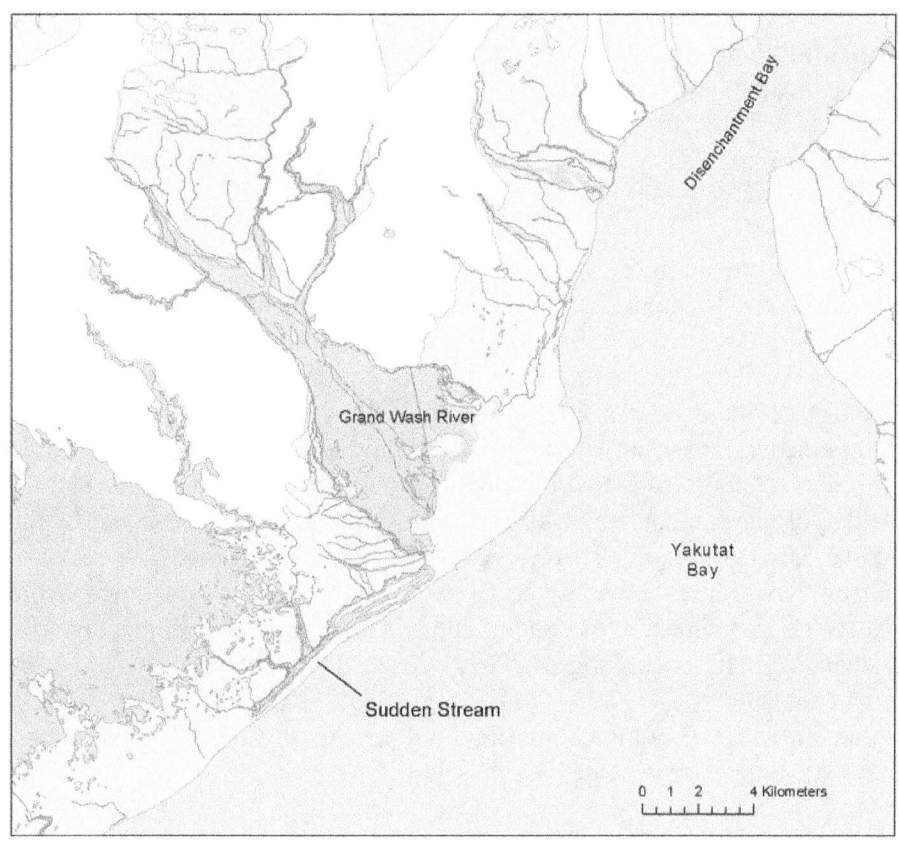

Figure 11. Location of Sudden Stream in Yakutat Bay. Two abandoned petroleum wells are located in close proximity to this stream.

After Alaska issued new solid waste regulations in 1987 requiring all oil field operators to provide closure plans for abandoned sites, British Petroleum Exploration (Alaska) Inc. (BPX), which had a "12.5 percent minority working interest in COGC", assumed responsibility for the clean up and monitoring of the Sudden Stream site (British Exploration (Alaska) Inc. 1991). The Sudden Stream remediation began in 1990, and 475 tons of drilling mud and debris were removed from the area (British Exploration (Alaska) Inc. 1991).

During the remediation, BPX discovered drilling mud reserve pits in the area. These were left undisturbed after it was agreed that performing corrective actions would only increase the impacts to the site (NPS. n.d. 1985-1992.). In 1988, the EPA originally submitted the site for Superfund consideration but due to inadequate information, it was never scored (Bleakley 2002). The EPA reviewed the site in 1995 and decided to include Sudden Stream on the National Priorities List (NPL), although based on the actions completed at the site, they assigned it a low priority for NPL listing (Bleakley 2002). In March of 1995, the ADEC approved the closure of the Sudden Stream site (NPS. n.d. 1985-1992.). Bleakley (2002) gives a detailed description of the discovery of contamination and cleanup of the Sudden Stream site.

B2b. ADEC listed contaminated sites

The ADEC lists two logging camps in Icy Bay as contaminated sites (Figure 10). The two logging camps are located on the west side of Icy Bay on State of Alaska lands, and have been in use since 1968. The camps use timber from State of Alaska lands, and are managed by either the University of Alaska or Department of Natural Resources Mental Health Trust Land Office.

In 2001, inspections of the facilities performed under the Forest Practices Act documented contamination that required remediation of the area. High concentrations of oil sheens and antifreeze were found along roadside ditches and personnel were observed releasing petroleum products into the environment from burning equipment and petroleum (DMC Technologies 2004). Groundwater from monitoring wells within both camps contained high concentrations of arsenic, beryllium, chromium, lead, and nickel. While petroleum hydrocarbons were not present in the wells, stream water samples collected near the two camps contained hydrocarbon concentrations four times the allowable level set by the Alaska Water Quality Standards (18 AAC 70). Two years later, clean up at the two sites was completed by using nine-genetically engineered bacterial strains that consume petroleum. Both reports state that the migration of contaminants is not expected to impact nearby streams and wetlands (DMC Technologies 2003; 2004).

More information on the Icy Bay log camps can be found on the ADEC website: http://www.dec.state.ak.us/spar/csp/sites/icy_bay.htm

B3. Sources of pollutants

B3a. Point source

Mining

Since the 1897 gold rush, considerable mining activity has occurred on valid mining claims within WRST over the years. Most mining activity has taken place in the northern, inland regions of WRST (NPS 1990). In fact, the majority of existing or historic roads and trails within the Park/preserve were constructed for access to mining or prospecting areas (NPS 1990). The Final Environmental Impact Statement, *Mining in Wrangell-St. Elias National Park and Preserve, Alaska*, analyzes the cumulative effects of past and future mining activities (NPS 1990). Although this report focuses on five study areas where the most mining activity has taken place-- the Nabesna, Chisana, Granite Peak, Kennicott, and Nizina areas-- past mining activity has also occurred in other parts of the Park (NPS 1990). Most mining operations were built in the first half of this century and are now abandoned. There are more than 400 known abandoned mineral and exploration sites in WRST (Weeks 2003). These abandoned sites often contain hazardous solid and liquid wastes, and these pollutants may impact water resources.

There is no documented historical mining activity in the coastal areas of WRST. However, it is highly possible that there were small-scale mining operations in the coastal areas of the Park. Although in the early 1990s there was some interest in mining placer beach sands along the coastline adjacent to the Park (personal communication, Danny Rosenkrans,

Geologist, Wrangell – St. Elias National Park and Preserve, 2005), today there are no mining operations in the coastal watersheds or coastal areas of WRST.

Oil and gas drilling

Petroleum is found in WRST owing to southeast Alaska's location next to an active plate boundary and its resulting complex structural geology. There is a correlation between oil seeps and seismicity, and the WRST coastline is a prime example of this phenomenon (Blasko 1976). Abundant oil and gas seeps were found in the Yakataga district around 1896 by prospectors exploring for gold, and currently there are 13 offshore petroleum wells in the Gulf of Alaska, just off the coastline of WRST, west and southwest of Icy Bay (Figure 12; US Department of the Interior 1992). Most of these offshore wells are exploratory wells drilled on Federal leases on the Outer Continental Shelf (OCS) (US Department of the Interior 1992). Onshore, oil seeps have been found in the Samovar Hills about 20 miles (32 km) east-northeast of Icy Bay (US Department of the Interior 1992). These onshore seeps are located between the Malaspina, Seward, and Agassiz glaciers and many seeps have been mapped along streambeds that are located along fault zones (Blasko 1976). So far, no producible hydrocarbons have been found either onshore or offshore.

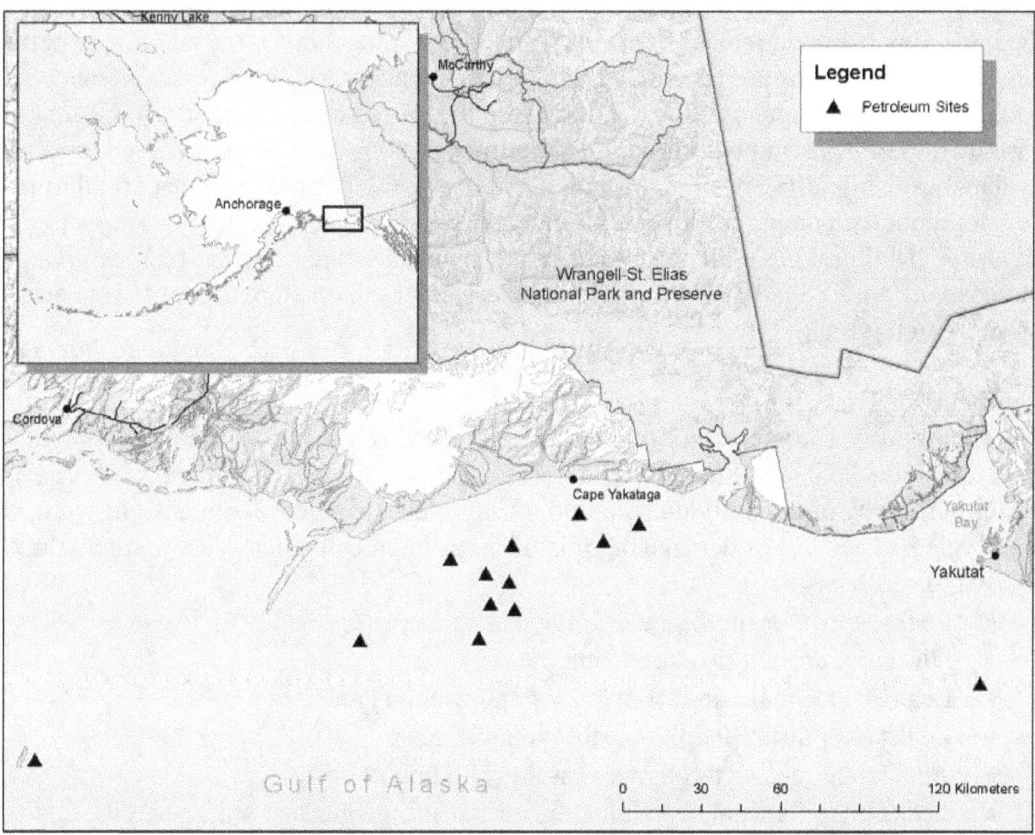

Figure 12. Location of thirteen exploratory petroleum wells in the Gulf of Alaska near coastal WRST.

Much like historic mining sites, abandoned drilling sites are often areas where hazardous solid wastes have been stored. These areas may have contaminants that could impact nearby surface and groundwater. Hazardous waste from one abandoned drilling site, Malaspina 1-A, has been found along the coastline of WRST, at Sudden Stream on the Malaspina Forelands (Figure 10). Sampling at the area showed elevated levels of barium and chromium in the water, soil and vegetation (Bleakley 2002). The Bleakley (2002) report provides a detailed description of the discovery of this contaminated site and the associated remediation actions. In 1995, after the successful clean up of this area, the ADEC approved the closure of the Sudden Stream site. More on the Sudden Stream site can be found in the "Water quality impairments" section of this report.

Because of the frequency of oil seeps in this area, it is highly likely that petroleum exploration will continue to occur both onshore and offshore along the coastline of WRST. The State of Alaska Department of Natural Resources Division of Oil and Gas has offered 350,000 acres (141,640 hectares) of onshore and offshore land up in a lease sale, the Cape Yakatage Sale 79. The area covered in this sale lies within a 3 mile (4.8 km) limit between Katalla and Icy Bay and includes the entire coastline of WRST (US Department of the Interior 1992).

Icy Bay is one of the only sheltered bays leased for petroleum exploration (Molnia 1978); thus, Icy Bay may be used as the primary onshore staging site for the support of petroleum development in the future. The unpredictability of many natural processes in this coastal area could impact development efforts. These include storm surges, tsunamis, large-magnitude earthquakes, glacial outburst flooding, shoreline erosion, sediment deposition, and snow avalanches (Molnia 1977, 1978, Molnia et al. 1979). Other processes that could impact development include permafrost melting, icebergs, shore-fast ice, icy gouging and glacial advances (Molnia 1978). These physical processes that affect this coastal area greatly increase the possibility of petroleum leaks and spills both onshore at the staging area and offshore in Icy Bay.

Petroleum spills
Petroleum poses a range of environmental risks when released into the environment, whether as catastrophic spills or chronic discharges. In addition to physical impacts of large spills, the toxicity of many of the individual compounds contained in petroleum is significant, and even small releases can kill or damage organisms. Petroleum can enter WRST waters through the following mechanisms:
- Leaks, spills, or discharge of bilge or ballast water.
- Discharge from a two-stroke engine.
- Leaks from small aircraft or ATVs that use the area.
- Leaks or spills at petroleum storage facilities.
- Accidental release through a vessel grounding or collision.
- Leaks or spills from abandoned historic drilling sites and storage areas
- Natural leaks from oil and gas seeps in the Gulf of Alaska

The impact of a release of petroleum from any of the above mechanisms would greatly depend on the size of the spill, the location of the spill, the type of petroleum product, and the effectiveness of the response to the spill. WRST's approximately 125 miles (201 km) of coastline along the North Gulf Coast of Alaska is used by large numbers of marine vessels, such as commercial fishing vessels, subsistence and sport fishing vessels, marine shipping traffic, and cruise ships. Because this coastal zone experiences some of the harshest marine weather conditions in the world, accidents that involve petroleum spills are possible. If a tanker or barge hauling hazardous substances were to have an accident, the high tidal range and strong currents could transport the spill a great distance and have disastrous effects (Weeks 2003). The resources management plan for WRST reports that marine vehicle accidents are common and recent shipping losses along the WRST coastline have included a luxury cruise ship, several barges, and many fishing vessels (NPS 1998). Other motorized traffic along the coastline of WRST includes small aircraft from subsistence hunters, researchers, and recreational users. Remote landing strips or hunting camps may have fuel storage tanks on the premises. Although the magnitude of spills from any of these individual sources may be small, together they may pose a cumulative threat to the environment.

Geographic Response Strategies (GRS), created through the ADEC and other agencies, are spill response plans tailored to protect a specific sensitive area from oil impacts following a marine vessel spill. There is a GRS for one selected site along the WRST coastline at Blizhni Point in Disenchantment Bay. The other two sites are closer to the community of Yakutat. These sites were selected based on the criteria of environmental sensitivity set forth in the Southeast Alaska Subarea Plan (ADEC 1997). Currently, there is no GRS available for Icy Bay. The ADEC Geographic Response Strategies for Alaska website states that even though a sensitive site may not have a GRS, this does not imply that the site should not be protected during an oil spill (ADEC 2005). GRS development can also benefit sites where no GRS are in place, because the tools and experience that are used to develop a GRS can also be transferred to non-GRS sites (ADEC 2005). If Icy Bay were to see increased cruise ship activity in the future, the potential for a leak or spill will increase and the area may need its own GRS.

Fecal coliform
Currently there is no evidence that WRST coastal waters are polluted by fecal coliform bacteria, but it is important to regularly monitor areas where people come in direct contact with the water. The Beach Environmental Assessment and Coastal Health (BEACH) Act, signed into law October 2000, states that coastal water monitoring should take place in areas used recreationally, and especially in areas that are close to a pollution source (EPA 2005)

Through surveys and community visits, the Alaska BEACH Grant Program has ranked public use beaches by their potential risk of being exposed to marine water polluted by fecal contamination by a variety of sources. Potential sources of fecal bacteria could be sewage, stormwater runoff, boating waste, malfunctioning septic systems, animal waste, and other sources. At this time, beaches in WRST have been ranked low risk by the Alaska BEACH Grant Program (personal communication, Barbara Smith, Alaska Department of Environmental Conservation, 2005). The coastal area of WRST is used for hunting, fishing, research and recreation purposes, although not in the large numbers that are seen by many other national parks. Coastal WRST is extremely remote and is not considered a high use area. Consequently, the threat of fecal coliform contamination affecting park users is small.

B3b. Non point source

Atmospherically-derived contaminants

The coastal region of WRST is generally considered to be a pristine area that is too remote to be affected by pollution activities in other parts of the world. However, evidence is mounting that Alaska and other arctic and sub-arctic regions are not immune from contamination by chemicals that are able to travel far from their original sources (Fitzgerald et al. 1998, Heiman et al. 2000, AMAP 2002, AMAP 2004). In fact, some of these chemicals not only can reach Alaska from distant sources in temperate and tropical regions, but they have a tendency to accumulate in Alaska. Entering the food chain, they biomagnify up trophic levels, and can pose serious threats to the health of marine, freshwater, and terrestrial organisms (EPA 2002).

Mercury and a group of chemicals known as Persistent Organic Pollutants (POPs) are the 2 major subjects of concern for Alaska in terms of global contaminants. Mercury, a strongly toxic heavy metal, is emitted primarily by fossil fuel burning (Pacyna and Pacyna 2002). POPs comprise a long list of highly toxic and very stable organic compounds such as polychlorinated biphenyls (PCBs), dichlorodiphenyltrichloroethane (DDT), dioxins, furans, and chlordane that are used as pesticides, industrial chemicals and industrial waste products (EPA 2002). While there are some localized sources for these chemicals, the vast majority of them are carried to Alaska via long-range atmospheric pathways (Strand and Hov 1996, Wania et al. 1999, Schroeder and Munthe 1998). Mercury and POPs in northern latitudes show significant concentration increases over the last few decades, and these trends are reflected in the extraordinarily high concentrations of some of these chemicals in the bodies of otters, whales, seals, bears, eagles, and indigenous peoples who rely on subsistence harvests (AMAP 2002, AMAP 2004).

Highly volatile POPs may travel directly to Alaska by long-range atmospheric transport, and less volatile POPs reach the region due to the "grasshopper effect", in which they are deposited and revolatilized in a successive northbound pattern (Wania and Mckay, 1996). Once deposited in the northern latitudes, they are slow to decompose due to the cold climate. Like some of the more volatile types of POPs, Hg accesses Alaska in a gaseous form. Gaseous Hg is highly volatile and sparingly soluble, and consequently, it can travel far distances and over long time periods (~1 yr) before being deposited (Schroeder and Munthe 1998, Petersen et al. 1995). Mercury deposition is particularly favored in high altitude and high latitude regions due to cold condensation processes (Schindler 1999). Anthropogenic mercury deposition to Alaska appears to be similar in magnitude to that in temperate latitudes (Fitzgerald et al. 2005). Elevated levels of methylmercury in fish have led to consumption advisories throughout most of the USA and much of Canada (EPA 2004, Pilgrim et al. 2000, Environment Canada 2004). However, little is known about the extent of Hg pollution in southeast Alaska.

Although Hg and POPs have not been studied in the WRST area specifically, several studies within southeast Alaska indicate the region as a whole is being impacted by these contaminants. One project evaluated the POPs and Hg concentrations in seabird eggs

(Christopher et al. 2002, Davis et al. 2004, Day et al. 2004), and the other examined the record of Hg in lakebed sediments in Glacier Bay National Park (GLBA) (Engstrom and Swain 1997).

Results of the seabird egg project showed that concentrations of POPs in common murre eggs from two islands in the Gulf of Alaska were significantly higher than in eggs from three colonies in the Bering Sea. Eggs from St. Lazaria (in Sitka Sound) had higher concentrations of SPCBs (sum of 46 congeners of PCBs) than eggs from any other Alaskan colonies. Samples from Gulf of Alaska colonies also showed that the contribution of 4,4'-DDE (dichlorodiphenyldichloroethylene) to the total concentration of POPs was twice as high as it was at the three Bering Sea colonies. Geographic differences in the POPs concentrations are not well understood, but they are thought to be products of global wind and ocean current patterns that result of variable deposition characteristics within Alaska. The same studies examining POPs in Alaskan seabird eggs also evaluated Hg concentrations (Christopher et al. 2002, Davis et al. 2004, Day et al. 2004). These studies indicate that mercury pollution may also be more of a concern in southeastern Alaska compared to other regions of Alaska. Murre eggs collected from islands in the Gulf of Alaska had mercury concentrations that were several-fold higher than in eggs from islands in the Bering Sea, and the highest concentrations of mercury were again from St Lazaria Island in the Sitka Sound (Figure 13). The authors of these studies speculate that the higher mercury concentrations in the Gulf of Alaska sites may be due to landscape characteristics in southeast Alaska (such as large areas of wetlands) that favor mercury methylation processes. More information on the seabird egg contaminant studies can be found at http://www.absc.usgs.gov/research/ammtap/stamp.htm

Figure 13. Mercury mass fraction (μg/g) in murre eggs (mean ± 95% confidence interval and corresponding median) plotted as a function of island location. East Amatuli Island is near the Kenai Peninsula and Saint Lazaria Island is in Sitka Sound. From Christopher et al. (2002).

The study of dated sediment cores collected at three lakes in GLBA suggests that modern Hg accumulation rates in sediments are approximately double pre-industrial accumulation rates (Engstrom and Swain 1997). Additionally, Hg deposition in GLBA did not show the recent declines (since the1960s) observed at sites in the continental US where regional mercury emissions have been reduced. These results suggest that southeast Alaska is being affected by mercury emissions from remote sources (e.g. in Asia), that are steadily increasing their output (Pacyna and Pacyna 2002).

The outlook is mixed for future deposition of POPs and Hg in southeast Alaska. The Stockholm Convention, a global initiative to phase out 12 of the most dangerous POPs should reduce the threat that these pollutants pose to ecosystems such as those within WRST. However, numerous other forms of POPs are still being manufactured and released into the environment in large quantities with unknown consequences (Giles 2004). The prospects for mercury contamination abatement are somewhat grim as well. While mercury emissions in the USA have decreased in recent decades, global emissions continue to increase, particularly in Asia, a major source region for prevailing weather patterns that feed the northwest coast of North America (Pacyna and Pacyna 2002). As a result, southeast Alaska is predicted to be impacted by rising mercury contributions for decades to come. In sum, the limited studies to date strongly suggest that the threats posed by mercury and POPs to ecosystems such as those in WRST in southern Alaska are significant and deserve further evaluation and monitoring.

C. Other Areas of Concern

C1. Marine Vessel Impacts

WRST's approximately 125 miles (201 km) of marine coastline along the Gulf of Alaska receives a fair amount of marine vessel traffic. The Gulf of Alaska is a major shipping route, and the region also sees traffic from commercial, sport, and subsistence fishing vessels and increasing water-borne tourism. Marine traffic also includes vessels and barges loaded with a wide variety of toxic materials, and fuel barges that regularly resupply local towns. WRST has some concern about increased cruise ship activity in Icy Bay, although as of yet there is no documentation of an increase in such traffic. Increased vessel traffic may directly or indirectly affect a variety of marine and coastal wildlife, flora, air and water quality, wilderness character, and the visitor experience.

There have been concerns by scientists and Native Alaskans who subsistence hunt in the area about the possible effects of tour vessels on marine life, especially marine mammals that are a subsistence resource for Native Alaskans. Jansen et al. (2003) studied the effects of cruise ships entering Disenchantment Bay on harbor seals that haul out on floating ice in the fjord, and found that when ships approached, seals were more likely to vacate ice floes and that there was a sharp increase in seals entering the water. This draft report (Jansen et al. 2003) also examined whether seals were more common in other coastal areas of WRST during times of high vessel use of Disenchantment Bay, however those results have not yet been released. Ice floes from tidewater glaciers serve as important pupping grounds for harbor seals from May to July (ADNR 1995), thus, it is necessary to understand how increased tourism will affect seal populations and survival.

C1a. Marine vessels impact on water quality

Marine vessels have the potential to degrade water quality in WRST by the accidental release of petroleum, the release of wastewater or other discharges, or by the resuspension of sediments (NPS 2003). The release of petroleum into the environment, whether as catastrophic spills or chronic discharges, could result in a wide range of environmental damage. The impact of a release of petroleum from a leak or spill in WRST would greatly depend on the size of the spill, the location of the spill, the type of petroleum product, and the effectiveness of the response to the spill. Petroleum spills are discussed in more detail in section B3a of this report.

Wastewater generated by marine vessels can also be a source of marine pollution. The types of wastewater that might be released into WRST waters include graywater (laundry, shower, and galley sink wastes), blackwater (treated sewage), hazardous waste, solid waste, and marine debris (NPS 2003). Hazardous wastes may include photo processing chemicals, dry cleaning or other chemicals, paint, cleaning solutions, pharmaceuticals, fluorescent lights and batteries. Solid wastes include food waste, plastic and glass containers, and paper products. The ADEC (2002) reports that dilution levels for small marine vessels that treat and continuously discharge their wastewater is extremely high, and that the only contaminant likely to be measured above ambient water levels would be fecal coliform. Private vessels may not be able to treat their wastewater before it is discharged. However, because of the small volumes of discharge and the large potential for dilution, the effects of wastewater released from small vessels should not be significant (NPS 2003).

Vessels can also affect water quality by resuspending sediments in marine waters through vessel movement. This can cause increased turbidity, which in turn decreases water quality by reducing light penetration and interferes with filter feeding organisms that are sensitive to turbidity (NPS 2003). The amount of resuspended sediment depends on the speed and size of the vessel, the sediment size, and the stability of the water column. Such effects to water quality in WRST are most likely temporary and limited to the immediate area of the vessels involved.

C1b. Marine vessels impact on underwater noise levels

All motorized vessels such as cruise ships, tour vessels, charter vessels, fishing vessels, private skiffs and even airplanes contribute to underwater noise levels in WRST. All marine vessels with propellers will produce propeller cavitation noise, and the narrowband and broadband noise produced is dependent on vessel and engine type (NPS 2003). Small vessels produce higher frequency noise due to their high speed engines and propellers. Large vessels produce substantial low frequency noise because of their size, slow speed engines, and propellers. Marine vessel noise may mask marine mammal communication signals (Erbe and Farmer 1998, Erbe 2003). Noise may disrupt echolocation signals by odontocetes (toothed whales) which may impede their ability to find prey or navigate. Noise may also disrupt a marine organism's reception of sound which is important in detecting surroundings, prey or potential predators. Additionally, noise pollution can disrupt normal behavior and, at high levels, may even induce physiological damage to tissues and organs.

C2. *Harmful Algal Blooms*

Harmful algal blooms (HABs) are caused by a few dozen phytoplankton that produce toxins. Although commonly called red tides, this term is misleading as with many HABs, there is no discoloration to the water, and many seaweeds produce colored blooms. HABs cause significant ecosystem, human health, and economic impacts (Anderson et al. 2000). HABs have become a national and international research focus in the past decade. Most areas of the world have some form(s) of harmful algal bloom, although the frequency, severity and diversity vary greatly. One thing that is certain is that HABs have been occurring more frequently and in more areas during the past few decades (Anderson 1995, Burke et al. 2000). HABs have caused mass mortalities of marine bird, mammal, and fish populations, and they cause a variety of human illnesses that vary by type of toxic phytoplankton or diatom. Some cause respiratory problems in humans in certain geographic regions. Southwest Florida, for example, now issues health alerts and suggests that people with certain health problems stay inside and away from beaches during certain blooms. HABs are known to cause a variety of shellfish poisoning (SP), including paralytic (PSP), diarrhetic (DSP), neurotoxic (NSP), and amnesic (ASP). A fifth human illness, caused by finfish and not shellfish, is Ciguatera Fish Poisoning (CFP).

Harmful algal blooms have been documented for centuries. Early records from explorers and hunters describe outbreaks of illness after men ate local shellfish that are most likely the result of ingesting intoxicated shellfish. First recorded deaths due to PSP occurred during exploration of Puget Sound and Strait of Georgia in 1791-1792 when several members of Capt. George Vancouver's crew died after eating shellfish from a cove near modern day Vancouver, BC. The earliest recorded event in Alaska was in 1799 when a party of Aleut hunters under the command of a Russian fur trading company ingested mussels. Within minutes, half the party experienced nausea and dry mouth, and two hours later, 100 hunters had died. Alaska has figured prominently in the discovery of HABs and associated toxins, as the family of toxins responsible for PSP were named saxitoxins because they were extracted from the butter clam *Saxidomus giganteus* from Peril Strait, just northeast of Sitka in Southeast Alaska.

The largest problem caused by HABs in Alaska is paralytic shellfish poisoning (PSP) from shellfish that have bioaccumulated the dinoflagellate *Alexandrium* (Figure 14). Alaska has one of the highest incidences of reported PSP in the world (Gessner and Schloss 1996). Paralytic shellfish poisoning can cause paralysis, gastrointestinal problems, and respiratory arrest and can be fatal if prompt medical care and respiratory support is not available. There is no antidote. People have died in Alaska from PSP as recently as a decade ago, and there is at least one human health incident per year. Since 1973, there have been 176 incidences of PSP in Alaska from 66 outbreaks, with the majority in Southeast Alaska (Figure 15, Gessner 1996).

Little is known about the distribution or abundance of PSPs in coastal areas of WRST. The Alaska Department of Environmental Conservation (ADEC) is responsible for testing shellfish for PSP. Due to the geographic extent of Alaska (50,000 miles of coastline) and the

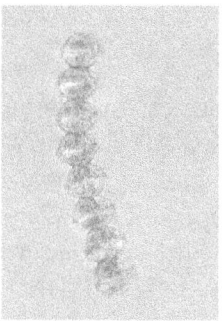

Figure 14. *Alexandrium*, the dinoflagellate responsible for PSP.

Figure 15. Location of PSP outbreaks in Alaska. Each star represents one or more outbreaks. Source: Gessner 1996.

remote nature of many regions of the state, shellfish are only tested for PSP in association with a commercial harvest or mariculture facility. Non-commercial harvests are not tested, and people are advised not to eat shellfish that they collect. More information is needed in order to evaluate if HABs are an issue of concern in WRST. Any unusual incidences of mass mortalities of marine bird, mammal, and fish populations should be suspected as possible HAB-related events.

C3. Invasive or Nuisance Species

The National Invasive Species Council, which was created by Presidential Executive Order 13112, defines invasive species as species that are "non-native (or alien) to the ecosystem under consideration and whose introduction causes or is likely to cause economic or environmental harm or harm to human health." The introduction of invasive species into Alaskan waters may be either accidental or due to negligence, and pathways of introduction include fish farms, aquaculture, transport on or in ballast water from ships or fishing vessels, live seafood trade, or sport fishing gear (ADFG 2002a). In order to minimize the impact of invasive species in Alaska, the Alaska Department of Fish and Game (ADFG) has developed an Aquatic Nuisance Species Management Plan (ADFG 2002a) with the purpose of focusing on preventing the invasion of those invasive species that are considered the highest threat. This plan can be found on the ADFG Invasive Species Website at http://www.adfg.state.ak.us/special/invasive/invasive.php.

We were unable to find any park-specific information on invasive species, and therefore the following discussion of invasive species applies generally to Southeast Alaska. Non-indigenous aquatic invasive species that have been introduced or are moving into Alaskan waters include multiple species of fish, plants, and invertebrates (Appendix E). Water bodies of Alaska are likely to be invaded by non-indigenous species because the temperature ranges of oceans, rivers and lakes vary much less than terrestrial temperature ranges (ADFG 2002a), however few invasions have been documented in aquatic systems in Southeast Alaska. Invasive fish species that have been introduced to some areas of Alaska include northern pike (*Esox lucius* (Linnaeus)), Atlantic salmon (*Salmo salar*), yellow perch (*Perca flavescens*), and various ornamental species. Northern pike are of great concern because they spread rapidly and cause widespread damage to resident species such as trout, grayling and salmon (ADFG 2002a). Farmed Atlantic salmon in Washington State and British Columbia are released into the North Pacific Ocean each year and may affect native populations through disease, colonization, interbreeding, predation, habitat destruction, and competition (ADFG 2002b). These farmed fish are thriving in the wild with recoveries in both British Columbia and Alaska. The first recorded catches of Atlantic salmon in Southeast Alaska occurred in 1991, and ADFG has documented over 700 recoveries of Atlantic salmon throughout Alaskan waters which represent an estimated 3,000 immigrants per year (ADFG 2002b). To date, Atlantic salmon have been caught in locations throughout Southeast Alaska including: Lynn Canal, Icy Strait, Ketchikan, Petersburg, and Yakutat (ADFG 2002b). Atlantic salmon pose a real threat to WRST, and although they have not yet been documented in the park, their appearance is likely.

The most likely invasive aquatic invertebrate species of concern is the green crab (*Carcinus maenas*) which is originally from northern Europe, became established in California in the 1990's, and has since become established in estuaries as far north as British Columbia (Appendix E). Bacteria, viruses, and parasites are also a threat to Alaskan waters because these can be easily introduced through nonindigenous species. Whirling disease (*Myxobolus cerebralus*), a parasitic infection in trout and salmon is present in all western states except Alaska and Arizona, and the likelihood of establishment in Alaska is poorly understood (ADFG 2002a). Various aquatic nuisance plants that are potential or actual threats in Alaska include hydrilla a/k/a water thyme (*Hydrilla verticillata*), dotted duckweed (*Landoltia (Spirodela) punctata*), purple loosestrife (*Lythrum salicaria*), Eurasian water-milfoil (*Myriophyllum spicatum*), reed canary grass (*Phalaris arundinacea*), Japanese knotweed (*Polygonum cuspidatum*), salt marsh cordgrass (*Spartina alterniflora*), dense-flowered cordgrass (*Spartina densiflora*), foxtail barley (*Hordeum jubatum*), and swollen bladderwort (*Utricularia inflata*) (Appendix E, ADFG 2002a).

C4. ATV use

All Terrain Vehicle (ATV) use is no longer legal in coastal WRST except as a method of accessing a few private inholdings and below the high tide line which is outside of NPS jurisiction. ATV use is mentioned as an issue of concern because of the great extent of ATV use in other areas of WRST and because of historical use of ATVs in coastal areas of WRST. Impacts to wildlife habitat from ATV use vary by type, season of use, ground conditions, intensity of use, and distribution. During the past three decades, the use of ATVs has increased dramatically in Alaska, especially for subsistence hunting and fishing. Research has shown that repeated ATV use can cause substantial environmental degradation, and is particularly of concern along wetlands, permafrost soils and steep slopes. Currently there are 182 mechanized trails in WRST covering 622 miles (1,001 km) (Weeks 2003). Studies of ATV use in WRST have documented impacts such as shifts in species composition, decreased cover of plant species, the melting of permafrost, erosion, and increased trail width (Cook 1990b). Additional research on ATV use in WRST found that the number of passes an ATV makes in an area is related to the severity of the impact on vegetation, soil and water (Racine and Ahlstrand 1985, Racine and Ahlstrand 1991). ATV use along stream channels can increase sedimentation and cause vegetative damage in the riparian zone, as well as altering the flow and structure of the stream (Weeks 2003). These impairments can degrade stream habitat and decrease fish production. The use of ATVs for subsistence hunting and fishing is no longer legal in the coastal region of the park and a previous evaluation of the impacts of ATV use in the Malaspina Forelands conducted in 1997 found that vehicular traffic was having little impact on coastal ecosystems (Thompson 1997). Of primary concern was the potential damage to the foredune community of beach wildrye, *Leymus mollis* (*Elymus mollis, E. arenarius*). The report noted that ATV traffic was restricted to the beach area below the foredune, and foredune crossing was restricted to established trails. Any future increase in ATV use to access inholdings or below the high tide line has the potential to damage sensitive coastal ecosystems such as wetlands, stream corridors, and intertidal areas.

C5. Physical impacts

Hazards associated with natural hydrological and geomorphic processes are found throughout WRST. Hazards in WRST include outburst floods, landslides, snow avalanches, advancing glacial systems, and seismic activity. Weeks (2003) discusses these natural processes in detail and makes recommendations for monitoring, predicting the timing of, and preparing for these hazards. Along the coastline of WRST, the geophysical hazards that have the greatest potential to impact water resources include: seismic activity, high rates of uplift, and the advance of Hubbard Glacier and associated flooding impacts around Russell Fjord.

C5a. Land surface uplift

Active tectonics in southeastern Alaska as well as the increased thinning of glaciers are contributing to the extremely high rates of land surface uplift (or isostatic rebound) in the region. Icefields in coastal southeastern Alaska have experienced rapid retreat and thinning in the last 100-200 years, and the rate at which ice is being lost appears to be increasing (Arendt et al 2002). The unloading of the earth's surface associated with this loss of ice has resulted in isostatic rebound of the earth's crust over a large area of southeastern Alaska (Hicks and Shofnos 1965, Clark 1977, Sauber et al. 2000, Larsen et al. 2004). Recent measurements of uplift in southeastern Alaska are among the highest ever recorded with rates of up to 25mm (0.98 inches) per year in Glacier Bay and 34 mm (1.34 inches) per year centered over the Yakutat Icefield, immediately south of WRST (Larsen 2003).

The active tectonic deformation of the southeastern Alaska region is also a possible source of uplift, however this effect is thought to be relatively minor compared to isostatic rebound (Larsen et al. 2004). The entire north Gulf of Alaska coast contains active fault systems associated with the juncture of the Pacific and North American tectonic plates. Tectonic events from seismic activity have played an important role in creating the physical environment of WRST coastline, even in recent years (Mills and Firman 1986). Seismic activity in Yakutat is high and has had five earthquakes with magnitude of 7.0 and higher between 1893 and 1975 (City of Yakutat 2005). In 1899 a series of major earthquakes in the Yakutat area (8.6 on the Richter scale) caused a broad area near Yakutat to be uplifted as much as 47 feet (14 meters) (Mills and Firman 1986).

Currently the land surface along the WRST coastline is being uplifted at as much as 12-24 mm yr^{-1} (0.5-0.9 inches yr^{-1}) (Figure 16). This uplift is altering the landscape of coastal WRST and causing dramatic changes in fisheries and wildlife habitat (Mills and Firman 1986). Uplift may cause changes in the composition and location of key vegetative types, and in the distribution of birds and wildlife along the coastline. For example, in many areas, high marsh communities dominated by grasses have replaced the sedge-dominated low marsh communities (Armstrong et al. 2004). Migrating birds such as pipits and longspur favor high marsh communities, while low marsh communities are nutritionally crucial for waterfowl such as Vancouver Canada Geese (Armstrong et al. 2004).

These ongoing shifts in the elevation of the land surface also have important implications for the hydrology of small coastal streams, many of which support salmon populations. Recent research in the Mendenhall Valley near Juneau has shown that water table levels have been decreasing at approximately 3.7 cm/yr (1.5 inches/yr) during the last two decades, likely as a result of land surface uplift (Walter et al. 2004). This decrease in the water table appears to be affecting the hydrology of streams within the valley. For example, during the last decade, Duck Creek, a small salmon stream, has experienced a steady decrease in low flows of approximately 0.003 m^3/s/yr (Walter et al 2004). As a result, the lower reaches of Duck Creek often now run dry in the spring and summer. The area around WRST is currently experiencing greater uplift rates than Juneau, thus it is possible that coastal streams fed by groundwater may experience similar reduced flows and become impassable for fish, limiting the range of certain anadramous stocks. The US Geological Survey office in Juneau is currently preparing a report on recent changes in the hydrology of Duck Creek resulting from land surface uplift (personal communication, Edward Neal, Hydrologist, USGS Juneau, 2005).

C5b. Hubbard Glacier

The Hubbard Glacier is located along WRST's coast on Disenchantment Bay at the head of Yakutat Bay (Figure 17). The Hubbard Glacier is the longest tidewater glacier in North America. It extends 122 km (76 miles) from Mt. Logan in Yukon Territory and the glacier's face is more than 9.6 km (6.0 miles) across and 90 m (295 ft) high.

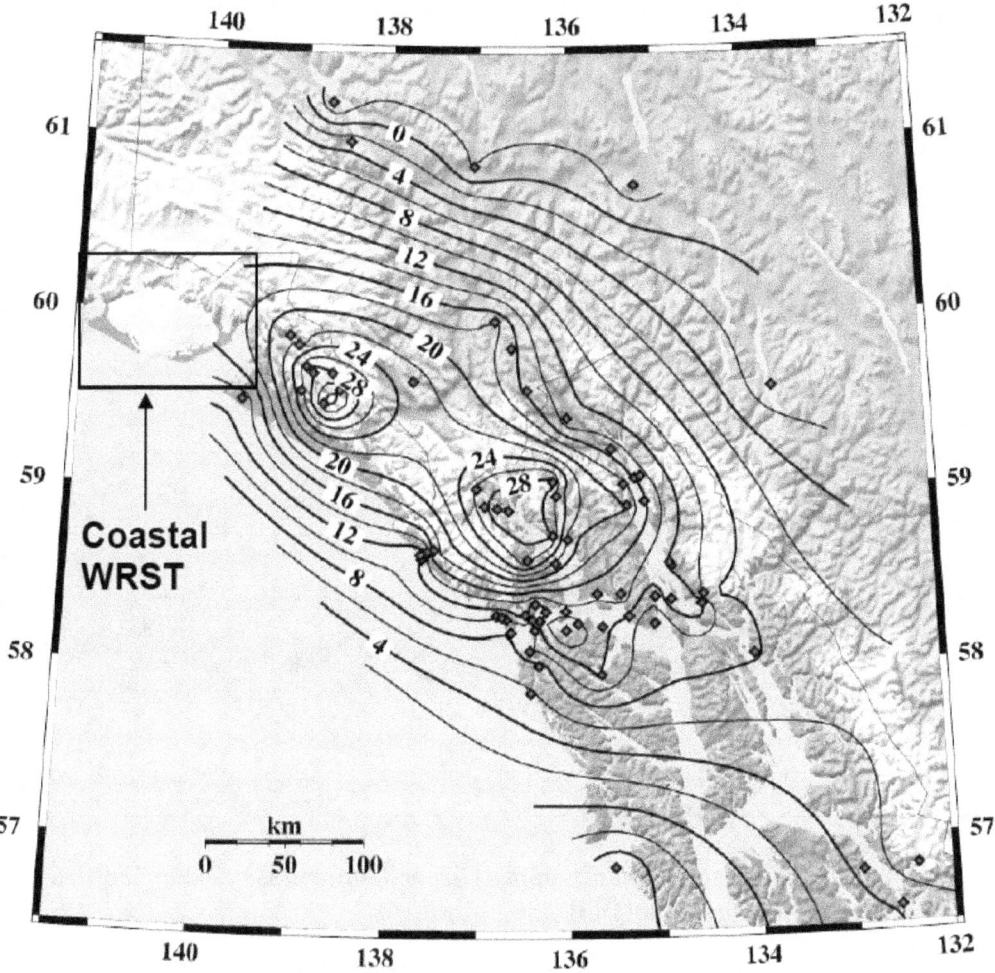

Figure 16. Land surface uplift rates in southeast Alaska (mm/year) from GPS measurements. Red diamonds are measurement sites. Modified from Chris Larsen, University of Alaska Fairbanks Geophysical Institute (http://www.giseis.alaska.edu/Input/chris/gpsuplift.jpg).

The Hubbard Glacier is not currently sensitive to moderate climate change. The Hubbard is in the advancing phase of the calving glacier cycle and has been advancing for more than 100 years. The current advance of the glacier is a hydrological hazard because the Hubbard has blocked the entrance to the 60 km (37 miles) long Russell Fjord twice in the last 20 years (in

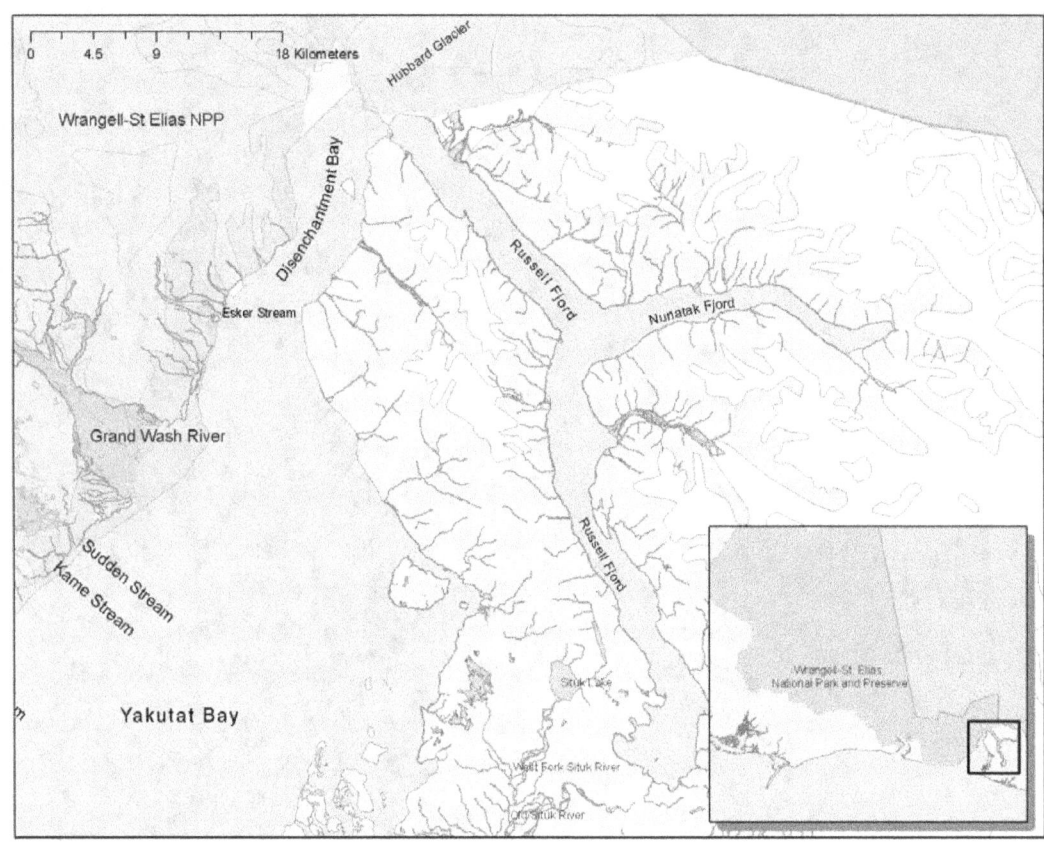

Figure 17. Location of the Hubbard Glacier in upper Disenchantment Bay. The Hubbard Glacier is threatening to create a dam at the outlet of Russell Fjord.

1986 and 2002) by squeezing and pushing submarine glacial sediments across the mouth of the Fjord (Trabant et al 2003a). The current advance of the Hubbard Glacier may again close the entrance to Russell Fjord, turning it into a freshwater lake. The glacial dam that formed in 1986 caused the surface of Russell Lake to rise more than 80 ft (24 meters) above sea level and the catastrophic failure of the dam released more than a cubic mile of water. The glacier dam that formed in 2002 only caused a rise in lake level of 49 ft (15 meters) (Figure 18). It is estimated that a 130 ft (40 meters) increase (relative to sea level) in the level of Russel Lake would cause water from the lake to spill over the confining topography and drain southward into the Situk River watershed outside the boundary of WRST (Weeks 2003; Trabant et al 2003b). This type of drainage event would have a dramatic impact on the town of Yakutat. The added flow from Russell Fjord would increase the average discharge of the Situk River by tenfold (Paul 1988), which would drastically alter the physical landscape in the Yakutat Forelands. In addition, the valuable Situk fishery, road systems, structures, and the Yakutat airport would all be adversely impacted (Motyka 2004).

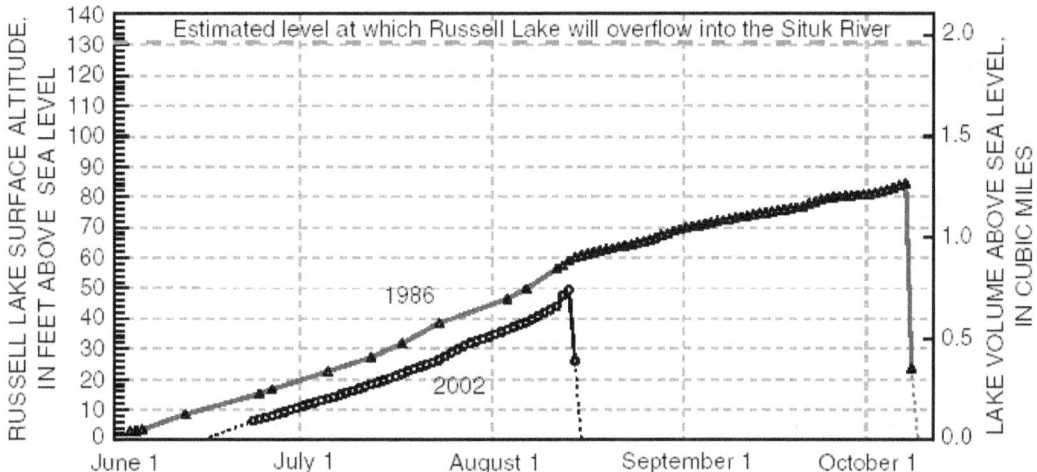

Figure 18. Lake level for Russell Lake during Hubbard Glacier dam events in 1986 and 2002The critical lake overflow threshold is shown at the top of the graph. From Trabant et al (2003b).

The US Forest Service, the National Park Service and the US Geological Survey have an ongoing research and monitoring program on the Hubbard Glacier. Information and data from this program are available at: http://ak.water.usgs.gov/glaciology/hubbard/index.htm

C6. Climate Change

Climate change is an important natural resource issue for national parks in Alaska (Weeks 2003), and recent research suggests that changes in climate may dramatically impact water resources in Alaskan parks. On a global scale, mean surface air temperature has risen by about 0.6 degrees Celsius (33.1 degrees Fahrenheit) in the last century and the best estimate of the International Panel on Climate Change is that temperatures will rise by another 1.7 to 4.0 degrees Celsius (35.1-39.2 degrees Fahrenheit) by 2100 (IPCC 2001). Recent climate change is dominated by human influences and there is now a relatively broad scientific consensus that the primary cause of climate change is human-induced changes in atmospheric composition (Karl and Trenberth 2003). In particular, there have been rapid increases in the concentration of greenhouse gases such as carbon dioxide and methane, which absorb and re-radiate outgoing terrestrial longwave radiation. Models and recent observations both suggest that climate warming is amplified at higher latitudes (Hall 1988, Mitchell 1989, Serreze et al. 2000). Thus future changes in temperature are projected to be proportionally higher in high-latitude systems (Roots 1989). Over the past fifty years, Siberia, Alaska and northern Canada, and the Antarctic Peninsula have warmed more than any other regions on Earth, and the 20th century arctic is the warmest of the past 400 years (Overpeck et al., 1997; Serreze et al. 2000). The reasons for the observed temperature increases at high latitudes are not fully understood, but are thought to involve cyospheric feedbacks, coupled with changes in the atmospheric circulation, and possibly ocean currents.

Climate warming is already affecting the physical landscape in Alaska. The most obvious effects of climate change on hydrologic resources in Alaska are changes in the extent of permafrost, snow cover, glaciers, and sea and lake ice cover (Oswood et al. 1992). Glaciers in both maritime and continental regions of Alaska are thinning and retreating at rapid rates (Arendt et al 2002). Currently glaciers in coastal WRST are thinning at rates as high as 4 meters (13 feet) per year (Figure 19). Losses of ice have been most dramatic at lower elevations along the coast, probably due to a warmer climate. Meteorological data from the nearby stations at Juneau, Sitka and Yakutat show a tendency toward an increase in average summer air temperature since 1943 when the meteorological record began (Motyka et al. 2003). Despite ongoing glacial retreat, some projections suggest that increasing winter temperatures in high-latitude areas may lead to greater snow accumulation (Mayo and Trabant 1984, Mayo and March 1990). Increases in snowfall could slow glacial retreat or even cause glacial advance. It is important to note that for glaciers in WRST, the effects of climate change may be very different for tidewater glaciers compared to glaciers that have a land-grounded terminus. The coastal region of WRST has numerous large mountain glaciers that are grounded and will respond closely to future changes in temperature and precipitation. In contrast, glaciers that terminate at tidewater follow their own cycles that are independent of short-term climate changes (such as the current advance of the Hubbard Glacier).

Glacial recession continues to shape the landscape of coastal WRST. During the past 200 years many of the glaciers along the coast have been retreating inland leaving bays along the Gulf of Alaska (Mills and Firman 1986). Both Yakutat Bay and Icy Bay have been enlarged since the 1800s as a result of receding glaciers (Mills and Firman 1986). Unlike most glaciers in WRST, the Hubbard Glacier is currently advancing into Disenchantment Bay and has advanced 2.5 km (1.6 miles) in the last century (Motyka 2004). As mentioned previously, the advance of the Hubbard Glacier poses a threat to Russell Fjord and the town of Yakutat, both of which are outside of park boundaries.

An important hydrologic effect of increased glacier melt is an increase in runoff from glaciers. Increased runoff can lead to the creation of new streams, and can alter the sediment, streamflow, and temperature regimes in surrounding streams (Oswood et al. 1992). Changes in runoff and sediment loads can change stream channel morphology and stability, as well as the composition of stream substrates and habitat complexity (Williams 1989). Reduced stream temperatures from increased glacial runoff can also decrease primary production, impact or eliminate certain invertebrates, and lower salmonid rates of production (Lloyd 1987, Lloyd et al. 1987). Over longer time scales, glaciers in WRST may produce less runoff as glacier mass decreases significantly (Benson et al. 1986).

Climate warming may affect the hydrology of terrestrial systems in WRST by causing areas of permafrost to thaw and dry out. This shift in the soil moisture regime would impact terrestrial ecosystems because the water-logged soils that make up permafrost contribute to the high diversity of plant life in many areas (Bruemmer 1987). Oswood et al. (1992) also suggests that the warming of northern soils may increase the carbon dioxide flux to the atmosphere which would exacerbate global warming. Thus, the loss of permafrost could increase carbon dioxide emissions from park ecosystems. Previous research has shown that melting permafrost can change shift tundra ecosystems from net sinks to net sources of carbon dioxide by facilitating the decomposition of soil carbon stocks locked up in permafrost (Chapin 1984, Billings 1987, Roots 1989).

It is also likely that climate change is affecting lakes and ponds within the coastal region of WRST. The area of small lakes and ponds within in WRST has decreased dramatically since the 1950's, with unknown effects on the species populations dependent on these waterbodies (Weeks 2003). Increasing air temperatures also have the potential to impact waterbodies such as high-altitude muskeg ponds and glacier-dammed lakes. The effects of climate change on the chemistry of lakes and streams is unknown. Research on linkages between terrestrial and aquatic systems suggests that elevated temperatures and carbon dioxide levels will affect the distribution and productivity of plants which will in turn affect the amount and quality of leaf litter entering streams and rivers (Meyer and Pulliam 1992). Sweeney et al. (1992) also suggest that there will be an increase in woody debris entering streams. Because soil microbial activity is linked to soil temperature and moisture, climate shifts will affect microbial processing of organic material in terrestrial systems. Overall, changes in inputs from terrestrial systems to lakes and streams will lead to shifts in litter decomposition rates (Webster and Benfield 1986), as well as changes in the productivity of heterotrophic and invertebrate populations (Anderson and Sedell 1979, Oswood et al. 1992). Stream water quality could also be altered by changes in the frequency of disturbances such as forest fires, wind storms, and coastal floods (Meyer and Pulliam 1992). Ultimately, changes to the quality and quantity of runoff from terrestrial ecosystems will affect near-shore marine systems in coastal WRST because the productivity of these systems is partially controlled by the input of nutrients from coastal watersheds.

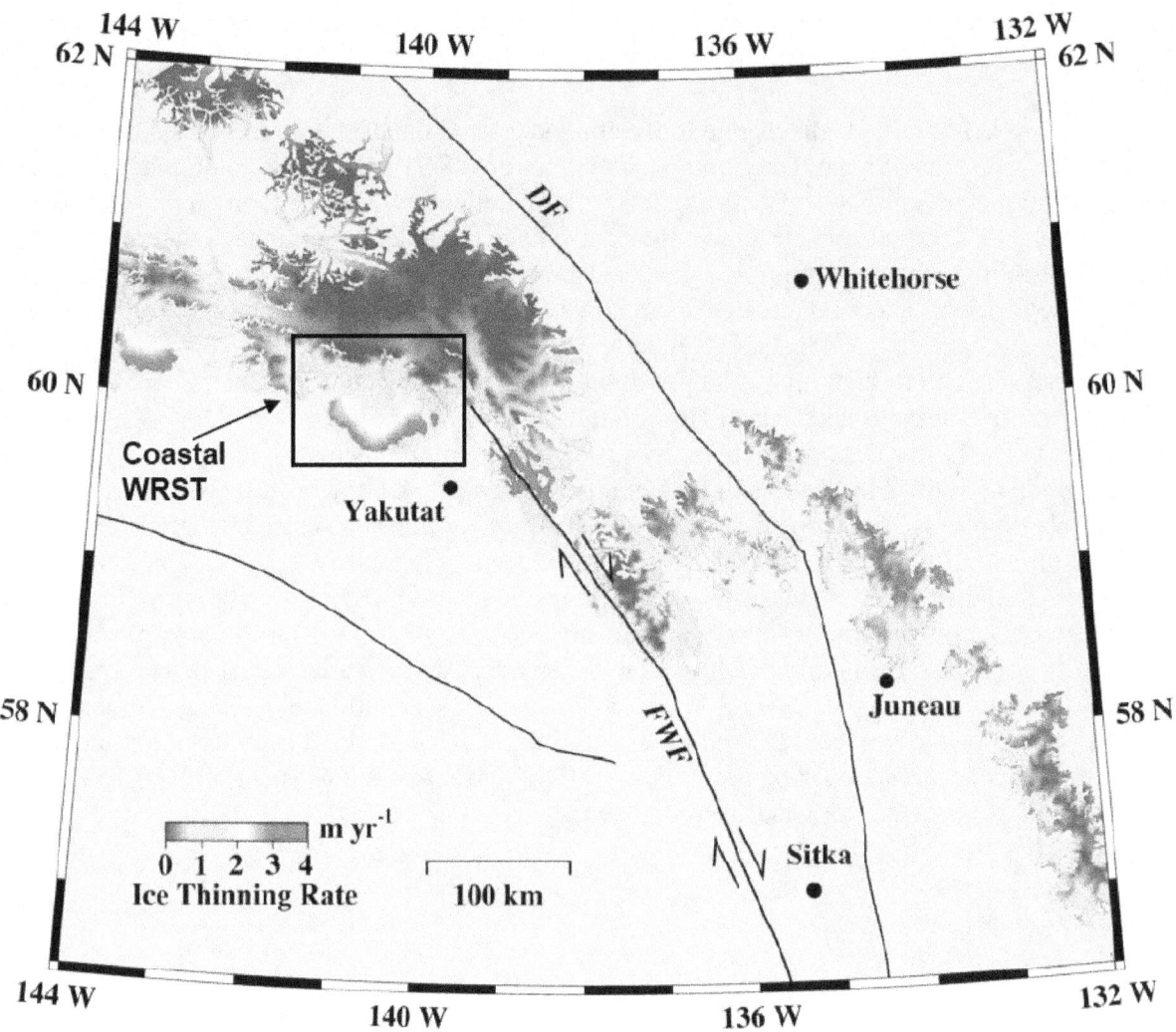

Figure 19. Current rates of glacier ice thinning in southeastern Alaska as measured by laser altimetry. Modified from Larsen et al. (2004).

D. Recommendations

D1. Condition overview

Table 3. Potential for impairment of coastal WRST water resources.

Indicator/Stressor	Upland/ Freshwater	Estuary	Marine/ Intertidal
Water Quality			
Eutrophication	OK	OK	OK
Contaminants	PP	OK	PP
Hypoxia	OK	OK	OK
Turbidity	OK	OK	OK
Pathogens	OK	OK	OK
Habitat Disruption			
Physical benthic impacts	OK	OK	OK
Coastal development	OK	OK	OK
Altered flow	OK	OK	OK
Erosion/Sedimentation	OK	OK	OK
Altered salinity	NA	OK	OK
Recreation/Tourism usage	OK	OK	PP
Other Indicators/Stressors			
Harmful algal blooms	NA	OK	PP
Aquatic invasive species	PP	PP	PP
Impacts from fish/shellfish harvesting	PP	OK	PP
Terrestrial invasive species	OK	OK	OK
Climate change	PP	PP	PP
Land surface uplift	PP	NA	NA

Definitions: EP= existing problem, PP = potential problem, OK= no detectable problem, shaded = limited, NA= not applicable.

D2. Recommendations

In writing this report, numerous data gaps were identified in terms of both freshwater and near-shore marine resources in the coastal region of WRST. The fundamental issue is that while the coastal area of WRST it vast and biologically rich, much of this area remains relatively unexplored. As a result, many of our recommendations relate to compiling information and establishing baselines.

Freshwater and Marine Resources

Water quality data are virtually non-existent for coastal waters and watersheds within WRST. Because of the remote location and low level of human activity, in particular mineral exploration and development, it is reasonable to assume that water quality within the coastal areas of WRST is in good condition. At the present time there is not a substantial threat to freshwater water quality from point sources of pollution in and around WRST. However, atmospheric deposition of pollutants does pose a threat to freshwater quality in coastal WRST. In addition, it is highly likely that the hydrology and chemistry of coastal watersheds will be altered by climate change and land surface uplift in the coming decades. The main threat to marine waters is pollution associated with marine vessels and petroleum spills.

Recommendations for management and monitoring freshwater and marine resources in WRST include:

- An inventory of streams, lakes, and other freshwater resources needs to be completed. The USGS National Hydrography Dataset provides detailed, high-resolution hydrologic information on waterbodies in coastal WRST (http://nhd.usgs.gov/) that would be useful for completing such an inventory. In addition, baseline characteristics on water chemistry, flow, flora, fauna, and aquatic habitats need to be collected for a representative set of streams in coastal WRST. This effort should be integrated into a regional water quality monitoring program.

- The majority of the wetland area in coastal WRST has been mapped, however mapping should be completed in northwestern portion of Yakutat Bay in a joint effort with the US Fish and Wildlife Service. In addition, the Hydrogeomorphic Approach Methodology developed by the ADEC should be used to assess wetland function and identify alternatives for management of wetlands in areas receiving substantial visitor use.

- Climate change is one of the major threats to water resources in Alaskan Parks. The hydrology of coastal parks such as WRST is particularly sensitive to climate change because the air temperature at sea level in southeastern Alaska is often close to the freezing point of water. As a result a relatively small increase in temperature can shift precipitation from snow to rain which, in turn, shifts the annual pattern of streamflow in these coastal systems. Basic physical parameters in coastal WRST should be monitored. Data collection should be automated and continuous, with transmittal of information to national databases (i.e. NOAA, USGS). Physical parameters that should be monitored include: sea level height, sea temperature, salinity, air temperature, precipitation, and other weather and oceanographic factors. WRST should install one or more automated climate stations in the coastal region of the park. This station or stations would provide baseline climate information and aid WRST resource managers in detecting future changes in climate.

- Measuring stream discharge should be a priority, particularly in one or more glacial watersheds. Discharge data can be used to evaluate present and future glacial influences on streamflow and can also be integrated into studies on glacial dynamics. At least one stream gaging station in the coastal region of the park should be established in partnership with the US Geological Survey.

- Rapid land surface uplift in coastal WRST has the potential to impact the physical and chemical characteristics of water resources, such as glaciers, lakes, streams, wetlands, and intertidal areas, as well as the health and distribution of vegetation, fish, and other wildlife. WRST staff should coordinate with Roman Motkya and Chris Larsen from the Geophysical Institute at the University of Alaska Fairbanks to expand their ongoing uplift monitoring program in Glacier Bay and Yakutat to include the coastal region of WRST.

- Local pollution sources are minimal; however, the concentration and distribution of global-scale pollutants such as mercury and persistent organic pollutants should be investigated and monitored in WRST's water and biological resources. Collecting and analyzing sediment cores from several lakes within WRST would allow for an assessment of the extent to which the deposition of global pollutants such as mercury is increasing within park boundaries.

- The cooperative effort to monitor the advance of the Hubbard Glacier which involves the US Forest Service, the US Geological Survey, and Wrangell-St. Elias National Park should be continued.

- The Alaska Department of Environmental Conservation is responsible for testing shellfish for PSP, however ADEC only tests for PSP in association with a commercial harvest or mariculture facilities. More information is needed in order to evaluate if shellfish poisoning associated with HABs are an issue of concern in WRST. NPS should advise against non-commercial harvests of shellfish because of the risks associated with PSP and should work with ADEC to conduct PSP testing on shellfish in coastal WRST.

- Invasive species within WRST in both marine and freshwater systems should be identified, monitored, and eradicated where feasible. A baseline survey of marine intertidal and freshwater resources in coastal WRST would serve this purpose and would provide valuable baseline data. Repeated surveys could be completed at intervals of 5-10 years.

- WRST should cooperate to continue wildlife surveys (e.g. surveys of marine mammals or birds by USFWS) as well as cooperate to ground truth ShoreZone surveys. NPS should obtain and archive this data (see data management below). NPS should provide resources to investigate populations that may be declining (e.g. harbor seals).

Human Utilization of Coastal WRST

Human use of coastal areas within WRST is not extensive, but it is increasing. Specific recommendations relevant to human use of WRST resources include the following:

- Human use, particularly in the form of tourism and recreation, is rising each year and should be documented. The spatial extent and intensity of subsistence hunting and fishing activities should also be quantified and monitored for future increases.

- Visitors use large and small marine vessels, small aircraft, and all-terrain vehicles (ATVs). With such motorized use comes an ever-present possibility of accidental fuel spills, leaks from fuel storage areas, and leaks from motorized vehicles themselves. Additionally, spills from petroleum product transportation by commercial marine vessels along the coastline of WRST are possible. The coastline and offshore area of WRST provide seasonal feeding, breeding, reproducing, and staging grounds for large numbers of migratory birds and marine and terrestrial mammals. Many of these wildlife populations function as important subsistence resources. WRST should identify critically sensitive areas and develop a plan of action in the event of a petroleum or fuel spill.

- Visitation by humans may bring disturbances to local wildlife that is sensitive to human presence, such as the pupping harbor seals in Icy Bay. To determine and mitigate such impacts, it is important to document baseline conditions, monitor wildlife populations, and educate visitors regarding sensitive locations and times of year for wildlife populations within the park.

- Petroleum development may occur in the future within the vicinity of coastal areas of WRST. Monitoring of the health of coastal ecosystems now will serve as a baseline to determine impacts of such development (see specific monitoring recommendations above).

- WRST should assess current levels of use by marine vessel traffic in the coastal region of the park. Understanding visitation rates and projecting potential future increases in use will allow managers to determine when it will be necessary to begin monitoring the effects of marine traffic on the quality of air and water (both chemical and noise pollution) along the coast.

Data access/management

- Online archives of NPS publications and reports - Obtaining information for this report was arduous and difficult, however information could be more readily obtained if NPS were to generate online archives of NPS publications and reports. Such an archive should be searchable. Historical documents should be entered to the extent possible.

- Integration of information into centralized and web-accessible GIS - Data from surveys, monitoring activities, impairments, and inventories should be integrated into a centralized and web-accessible GIS.

References

ADEC. 1997. Southeast Subarea Contingency Plan for Oil and Hazardous Substance Spills and Releases. A subarea plan of the Unified Plan for the State of Alaska. Alaska Department of Environmental Conservation, State of Alaska.

ADEC. 2002. Science Advisory Panel, Commercial Passenger Vessel Environmental Compliance Program. The Impact of Cruise Ship Wastewater Discharge on Alaska Waters. Alaska Department of Environmental Conservation.

ADEC. 2003. Alaska's Final 2002/2003 Integrated Water Quality Monitoring and Assessment Report. Alaska Department of Environmental Conservation.

ADEC. 2005. Geographic Response Strategies for Southeast Alaska http://www.dec.state.ak.us/spar/perp/grs/se/home.htm. Alaska Department of Environmental Conservation. State of Alaska.

ADFG. 2002a. Alaska Aquatic Nuisance Species Management Plan. Alaska Department of Fish and Game, Juneau, AK.

ADFG. 2002b. Atlantic Salmon - A White Paper. Alaska Department of Fish and Game, Commissioner's Office, Juneau, Juneau, AK.

ADFG. 2005. Catalog of Waters Important for the Spawning, Rearing and Migration of Anadromous Fishes. State of Alaska, Department of Fish and Game, Habitat Division, Juneau, AK.

ADNR. 1995. Yakataga Area Plan. Alaska Department of Natural Resources, Division of Land Resource Assessment & Development Section, Anchorage, AK.

AMAP. 2002. AMAP Assessment Report: Arctic Pollution Issues: Persistent Organic Pollutants, Heavy Metals, Radioactivity, Human Health, Changing Pathways. Arctic Monitoring and Assessment Programme (AMAP), Oslo, Norway.

AMAP. 2004. AMAP Assessment Report: Arctic Pollution Issues: Persistent Organic Pollutants, Heavy Metals, Radioactivity, Human Health, Changing Pathways. Arctic Monitoring and Assessment Programme (AMAP), Oslo, Norway.

Anderson, D. M. 1995. ECOHAB: The Ecology and Oceanography of Harmful Algal Blooms - A National Research Agenda. WHOI, Woods Hole, MA.

Anderson, D. M., P. Hoagland, Y. Kaoru, and A. W. White. 2000. Estimated Annual Economic Impacts from Harmful Algal Blooms (HABs) in the United States. WHOI-2000-11, Woods Hole Sea Grant, Woods Hole, MA.

Anderson, N. H., and J. R. Sedell. 1979. Detritus procession by macroinvertebrates in stream ecosystems. Annnual Review of Entomology **24**:351-377.

Andres, B. A., and B. T. Browne. 1998. Spring migration of shorebirds on the Yakutat Forelands, Alaska. Wilson Bulletin **110**:326.

Arendt, A. A., K. A. Echelmeyer, W. D. Harrison, C. S. Lingle, and V. B. Valentine. 2002. Rapid wastage of Alaska Glaciers and Their Contribution to Rising Sea Level. Science **29**: 382-386.

Arimitsu, M. L., Michael A. Litzow, John F. Piatt, Martin D. Robards, Alisa A. Abookire, Gary S. Drew. 2003. Inventory of Marine and Estuarine Fishes in Southeast and Central Alaska National Parks. USGS.

Armstrong, R. H., R. L. Carstensen, and M. F. Willson. 2004. Hotspots: Bird Survey of Mendenhall Wetlands, April 2002 to May 2003. Juneau Audubon Society and Taku Conservation Society, Juneau, AK.

Back, W., J. S. Rosenshein, and P. R. Seaber. 1988. Hydrogeology. The Geological Society of America, Inc., Boulder, CO.

Beck, K. A. 1989. Icy Bay Glacial Succession Monitoring Draft Progress Report. National Park Service, Wrangell-St. Elias National Park and Preserve, AK.

Benson, C., W. Harrison, J. Gosnik, S. Bowling, L. Mayo, and D. Trabant. 1986. Workshop on Alaskan Hydrology: Problems related to glacierized basins. Geophysical Institute Report UAG-R (306), University of Alaska Fairbanks, Fairbanks, AK.

Betts, M. F., M. Kookesh, R. F. Shroeder, T. F. Thornton, and A. M. Victor. 1999. Subsistence resource use patterns in Southeast Alaska: Summaries of 30 communities, Yakutat. Alaska Department of Fish and Game, Division of Subsistence, Juneau, AK.

Bilby, R. E., B. R. Fransen, and P. A. Bisson. 1996. Incorporation of nitrogen and carbon from spawning coho salmon into the trophic system of small streams: evidence from stable isotopes. Canadian Journal of Fisheries and Aquatic Sciences **53**:164-173.

Billings, W. D. 1987. Carbon balance of Alaskan tundra and taiga ecosystems: Past, present and future. Quaternary Science Reviews **6**:165-177.

Blasko, D. P. 1976. Occurrences of oil and gas seeps along the Gulf of Alaska. Pages 211-220 *in* Anonymous, editor. Presented at: 8. Annual Offshore Technology Conference, Houston, TX (USA), 3 May 1976.

Bleakley, G. T. 2002. Contested Ground: An Administrative History of Wrangell-St. Elias National Park and Preserve, Alaska 1978-2001. National Park Service, Alaska Systems Support Office, Anchorage, AK.

Bograd, S.J., P.J. Stebeno, and J.D. Schumacher. 1994. A census of mesoscale eddies in Shelikof Strait, Alaska, during 1989. Journal of Geophysical Research. 99: 18,243-18,254

British Exploration (Alaska) Inc. 1991. Malaspina Unit No. 1 A. Core Hole No. 2. Cole Hore No. 4.Surface Debris Clean-Up Program, October 1, 1991.

Bruemmer, F. 1987. Life upon the permafrost. Natural History **96**:30-39.

Bryant, M. D., and F. H. Everest. 1998. Management and Condition of Watersheds in Southeast Alaska: The Persistence of Anadromous Salmon. Northwest Science **72**:249.

Burke, L., Y. Kura, K. Kassem, C. Revenga, M. Spaulding, and D. McAllister. 2000. Pilot Analysis of Global Ecosystems (PAGE): Coastal Ecosystems. World Resources Institute, Washington DC

Calkins, D. G., D. C. McAllister, K. W. Pitcher, and G. W. Pendleton. 1999. Steller sea lion status and trend in Southeast Alaska: 1979-1997. Marine Mammal Science **15**:462-477.

Cederholm, C. J., M. D. Kunze, T. Murota, and A. Sibatani. 1999. Pacific salmon carcasses: Essential contributions of nutrients and energy for aquatic and terrestrial ecosystems. Fisheries **24**:6-15.

Chaloner, D. T., and M. S. Wipfli. 2002. Influence of Decomposing Pacific Salmon Carcasses and Macroinvertebrate Growth and Standing Stock in Southeastern Alaska Streams. Journal of the North American Benthological Society **21**:430-442.

Chapin, F. S. 1984. The impact of increased air temperature on tundra plant communities. Pages 143-146 *in* J. H. McBeath, G. P. Juday, G. Weller, and M. Murray, editors. The Potential Effects of Carbon Dioxide-Induced Climatic Changes in Alaska. School of Agriculture and Land Resources Management, University of Alaska Miscellaneous Publication 83-1, Fairbanks, AK.

Christopher, S. J., S. S. Vander Pol, R. S. Pugh, D. Day, and P. R. Becker. 2002. Determination of mercury in the eggs of common murres (Uria aalge) for the seabird tissue archival and monitoring project. Journal of Analytical Atmoic Spectrometry **17**:780-785.

City of Yakutat. 2005. Greater Yakutat Chamber of Commerce webpage. Last accessed: June 02, 2005

Clark, J. A. 1977. An inverse problem in glacial geology: The reconstruction of glacier thinning in Glacier Bay, Alaska between A.D. 1910 and 1960 from relative sea level data. Journal of Glaciology **18**:481-403.

Cook, M. B. 1988. Sudden Stream Vegetation Survey and Sampling for Barium and Chromium. Wrangell-St. Elias National Park and Preserve, National Park Service, Yakutat, AK.

Cook, M. B. 1990a. Field survey of Icy Bay Mine Site. Wrangell-St. Elias National Park and Preserve. National Park Service.

Cook, M. B. 1990b. Monitoring report for access to mine claims in the Gold Hill areas in Wrangell-St. Elias National Park and Preserve. Unpublished report. Wrangell-St. Elias National Park and Preserve, Glennallen, AK.

Crawford, W.R., Cherniawsky, J.Y., Foreman, M.G. and Gower, J.F.R. 2002. Formation of the Haida-1998 oceanic eddy. Journal of Geophysical Research 107:10,1029

Davis, W. C., S. S. Vander Pol, M. M. Schantz, S. E. Long, R. D. Day, and S. J. Christopher. 2004. An accurate and sensitive method for the determination of methylmercury in biological specimens using GC-ICP-MS with solid phase microextraction. Journal of Analytical Atmoic Spectrometry **19**:1546-1551.

Day, R. D., S. J. Christopher, S. S. Vander Pol, R. S. Pugh, and P. R. Becker. 2004. Seabird eggs as indicators of mercury contamination in the Alaskan marine environment. Proceedings of the International Conference on Environmental Science and Technology.

de Laguna, F. 1972. Under Mount Saint Elias: The History and Culture of the Yakutat Tlingit. Smithsonian Contribution to Anthropology **7**.

DMC Technologies. 2004. Revised final cleanup report, Icy Bay West Camp #1. Volume 1. Prepared for State of Alaska, Department of Environmental Conservation, Juneau, AK.

Doroff, A., and C. Gorbics. 1998. Sea otter surveys of Yakutat Bay and Adjacent Gulf of Alaska Coastal Areas - Cape Hinchinbrook to Cape Spencer 1995-1996. Marine Mammals Management, US Fish and Wildlife Service, Anchorage, AK.

Dyurgerov, M. B., and M. F. Meier. 2000. Twentieth century climate change: Evidence from small glaciers. Proceedings of the National Academy of Science **97**:1406-1411.

Engstrom, D. R., and E. B. Swain. 1997. Recent declines in atmospheric mercury deposition in the upper midwest. Environmental Science and Technology **31**:960-967.

ENSR Consulting and Engineering. 1991. Sudden Stream Site. Yakutat Alaska. Post-Cleanup Monitoring, 1990.

Environment Canada. 2004. Mercury and the environment: Fish consumption. http://www.ec.gc.ca/MERCURY/EN/fc.cfm#BC. Last accessed: July 11, 2005

EPA. 2002. Persistent Organic Pollutants: A Global Issue, A Global Response. http://www.epa.gov/oiamount/toxics/pop.htm#pops. Last accessed: July 15, 2005

EPA. 2005. Alaska BEACH Grant Program Webpage. http://www.state.ak.us/dec/water/wqsar/wqs/beachprogram.htm. Last accessed: February 7, 2005

Erbe, C. 2003. Assessment of Bioacoustic Impact of Ships on Humpback Whales in Glacier Bay, Alaska. National Park Service, Gustavus, Alaska.

Erbe, C., and D. M. Farmer. 1998. Masked Hearing Thresholds of a Beluga Whale (Delphinapterus leucas) in Icebreaker Noise. Deep-Sea Research II **45**:1373-1388.

Fitzgerald, W. F., D. R. Engstrom, C. H. Lamborg, C. M. Tseng, P. H. Balcom, and C. R. Hammerschmidt. 2005. Modern and historic atmospheric mercury fluxes in northern Alaska: Global source and arctic depletion. Environmental Science and Technology **39**:557-568.

Fitzgerald, W. F., D. R. Engstrom, R. P. Mason, and E. A. Nater. 1998. The case for atmospheric mercury contamination in remote areas. Environmental Science and Technology **32**:1-7.

Fountain, A. G., R. B. Schlicting, R. W. Jacobel, and P. Jansson. 2005. Fractures as main pathways of water flow in temperate glaciers. Nature **433**:618-621.

Gelatt, T., A. Trites, K. Pitcher, K. Hastings, and L. Jemison. 2004. Steller sea lion population trends, diet, and brand-resighting observations in Glacier Bay. *in* Glacier Bay Science Symposium. National Park Service, Juneau, AK.

Gende, S. M., R. T. Edwards, M. F. Willson, and M. S. Wipfli. 2002. Pacific salmon in aquatic and terretrial ecosystems. BioScience **52**:917 - 926.

Gessner, B. D. 1996. Epidemiology of paralytic shellfish poisoning outbreaks in Alaska. Alaska's Marine Resources **8**:16-17.

Gessner, B. D., and M. Schloss. 1996. A population-based study of paralytic shell fish poisoning in Alaska. Alaska Medicine **38**:54-58.

Giles, J. 2004. Treaty calls time on long term pollutants. Nature **247**:768.

Hall, D. K. 1988. Assessment of climate change using satellite technology. Reviews of Geophysics **26**:26-39.

Hare, S.R., N.J. Mantua, and R.C. Francis. 1999. Inverse production regimes: Alaska and west coast Pacific salmon. Fisheries. 24: 6-14.

Heiman, M., M. Brown, J. Middaugh, J. Berner, P. Cochran, M. Davis, S.Marcy, C. Hild, P. Johnson, J. Hohn, P. Miller, B. Wang, B. Wright, and M. Bradley. 2000. Contaminants in Alaska: Is America's Arctic at Risk? A white paper published by the Department of the Interior and the State of Alaska. Avaliable at http://www.conservationinstitute.org/contaminantsinalaska.htm.

Helfield, J. M., and R. J. Naiman. 2001. Effects of salmon-derived nitrogen on riparian forest growth and implications for stream productivity. Ecology **82**:2403-2409.

Hicks, S. D., and W. Shofnos. 1965. The determination of land emergence from sea-level observations in southeast Alaska. Journal of Geophysical Research **70**:3315-3320.

Hood, D.W. 1986. Physical Setting and Scientific History. In D.W. Hood and S.T. Zimmerman Eds. The Gulf of Alaska: Physical Environment and Biological Resources. NOAA Ocean Assessment Division, Alaska Office, Washington, D.C.

Hubbard, J. D., D. J. Hansen, and B. A. Mahoney. 1999. Winter sighting of beluga whales (Delphinapterus leucas) in Yakutat-Disenchantment Bay, Alaska. Arctic **52**:411-412.

Incze, L.S., A.W. Kendall, J.D. Schumacher, and R.K. Reed. 1989. Interactions of a mesoscale patch of larval fish (*Theragra chalcogramma*) with the Alaska Coastal Current. Continental Shelf Research. 9: 269-284.

IPCC. 2001. IPCC Third Assessment Report-Climate Change 2001: The Scientific Basis. http://www.ipcc.ch/pub/online.htm. Last accessed: Last accessed: July 1, 2005

Jaeger, J. M., and C. A. Nittrouer. 1999. Sediment deposition in an Alaskan Fjord: Controls on the formation and preservation of sedimentary structures in Icy Bay. Journal of Sedimentary Research **69**:1011-1026.

Jansen, J. K., J. L. Bengtson, P. L. Boveng, and S. P. Dahle. 2003. Investigation of the potential disturbance of harbor seals by cruise ships in Disenchantment Bay, Alaska, May to August 2002. Draft report National Marine Mammal Laboratory, Alaska Fisheries Science Center, NOAA Fisheries.

Johnston, N. T., E. A. MacIsaac, P. J. Tschaplinski, and K. J. Hall. 2004. Effects of the abundance of spawning sockeye salmon (Oncorhynchus nerka) on nutrients and algal biomass in forested streams. Canadian Journal of Fisheries and Aquatic Sciences **61**:384-403.

Jones, S. H., and R. L. Glass. 1993. Hydrologic and Mass-Movement Hazards near McCarthy, Wrangell-St Elias National Park and Preserve, Alaska. Pages 55 *in*. US Geological Survey. Water-Resources Investigations Report 93-4078, Anchorage, AK.

Karl, T. R., and K. E. Trenberth. 2003. Modern Global Climate Change. Science **302**.

Kozie, K. 1993. Coastal Wildlife Survey - Seabirds and Marine Mammals along the Malaspina Forelands 1992. Water Research and Resource Management Report No. 92-07. Wrangell-St. Elias National Park and Preserve, National Park Service.

Kozie, K., M. Kralovek, and R. Yerxa. 1996. Icy Bay Seabird Census in Wrangell-St. Elias National Park and Preserve, 1995. National Park Service.

Larsen, C. F. 2003. Rapid uplift of southern Alaska caused by recent ice loss. Masters Thesis. University of Alaska Fairbanks, Fairbanks, Alaska.

Larsen, C. F., R. J. Motyka, J. T. Freymueller, K. A. Echelmeyer, and E. R. Ivins. 2004. Rapid uplift of southern Alaska caused by recent ice loss. Geophysical Journal International **158**:1118-1133.

Lloyd, D. S. 1987. Turbidity as a water quality standard for salmonid habitats in Alaska. North American Journal of Fisheries Management **7**:34-45.

Lloyd, D. S., J. P. Koenings, and J. D. LaPerriere. 1987. Effects of turbidity in fresh waters of Alaska. North American Journal of Fisheries Management **7**:18-33.

Markis, J., E. Veach, and M. McCormick. 2004. Freshwater Fish Inventory of Denali National Park and Preserve, Wrangell St. Elias National Park and Preserve, and Yukon-Charley Rivers National Park and Preserve. Central Alaska Inventory and Monitoring Network. Alaska Inventory and Monitoring Program, National Park Service, Alaska Region.

Mathews, E. A., and B. P. Kelly. 1996. Extreme temporal variation in harbor seal (Phoca vitulina richardsi) numbers in Glacier bay, a glacial fjord in southeast Alaska. Marine Mammal Science **12**:483-489.

Mathews, E. A., and G. W. Pendleton. 2000. Declining trends in harbor seal (Phoca vitulina richardsi) numbers at glacial ice and terrestrial haulouts in Glacier Bay National Park, 1992-1998.24.

Mayo, L., and D. C. Trabant. 1984. Observed and predicted effects of climate change on Wolverine Glacier, southern Alaska. Pages 114-123 *in* J. H. McBeath, G. P. Juday, G. Weller, and M. Murray, editors. The Potential Effects of Carbon Dioxide-Induced Climate Change in Alaska. School of Agriculture and Land Resources Management, University of Alaska Miscellaneous Publications 83-1.

Mayo, L. R., and R. S. March. 1990. Air temperature and precipitation at Wolverine Glacier, Alaska; Glacier growth in a warmer, wetter climate. Ann. Glaciol. **14**:191-194.

Meyer, J. L., and W. M. Pulliam. 1992. Modification of terrestrial-aquatic interactions by a changing climate. Pages 177-191 *in* P. Firth and S. G. Fisher, editors. Global Climate Change and Freshwater Ecosystems. Springer-Verlag, New York.

Mills, D. D., and A. S. Firman. 1986. Fish and Wildlife Use in Yakutat Alaska: Contemporary Paterns and Changes. Alaska Department of Fish and Game, Division of Subsistence, Douglas, AK.

Mitchell, J. F. B. 1989. The "greenhouse" effect and climate change. Reviews of Geophysics **27**:115-139.

Mitchell, N. L., and G. A. Lamberti. 2005. Responses in dissolved nutrients and epilithon abundance to spawning salmon in Southeast Alaska streams. Limnology and Oceanography **50**:217-227.

Molnia, B. 2001. Glaciers of Alaska. Alaska Geographic **28**.

Molnia, B. F. 1977. Rapid shoreline erosion and retreat at Icy Bay, Alaska - A staging area for offshore petroleum development. *in* Offshore Technology Conference. US Geological Survey, Houston, Texas, May 2-5, 1977.

Molnia, B. F. 1978. Impact of coastal processes on resource development with an example from Icy Bay, Alaska. *in* Circum-Pacific Energy and Minerals Conference. US Geological Survey, Honolulu, Hawaii.

Molnia, B. F., V. Goldsmith, H. F. Hennigar, A. L. Gutman, and N. T. Blake. 1979. Sedimentation in coastal embayments, northeastern Gulf of Alaska. *in* Offshore Technology Conference, Houston, TX (USA), 30 Apr 1979.

Motyka, R. J. 2004. Hubbard Glacier, Alaska: the 2002 closure of Russell Fjord and the potential for future closures based on glacier dynamics and fjord bathymetry. Unpublished work. University of Alaska Fairbanks, Fairbanks, AK.

Motyka, R. J., L. Hunter, K. A. Echelmeyer, and C. Connor. 2003. Submarine melting at the terminus of a temperate tidewater glacier, LeConte Glacier, Alaska. Annals of Glaciology **36**:57-65.

Mundy, P.R., and P. Olsson. 2005. Climate and Weather. In P.R. Mundy, Ed. The Gulf of Alaska: Biology and Oceanography. Alaska Sea Grant College Program, Universty of Alaska Fairbanks.

Muskett, R. R., C. S. Lingle, W. V. Tangborn, and B. T. Rabus. 2003. Multi-decadal elevation changes on Bagley Ice Valley and Malaspina Glacier, Alaska. Geophysical Research Letters **30**.

NPS. 1986. General Park Management Plan (http://www.nps.gov/wrst/GMP1986/GMP.htm). Wrangell-St. Elias National Park, National Park Service.

NPS. 1990. Mining in Wrangell-St. Elias National Park and Preserve, Alaska. Final Environmental Impact Statement. Vol.1. National Park Service, Anchorage, AK.

NPS. 1992. David Shaver to Alaska Regional Director, NPS, July 6, 1992, Sudden Stream Hazardous Waste Site folder 1992, Environmental files. Wrangell-St. Elias National Park.

NPS. 1994. Water quality surveys of Copper, Ptarmigan, and Tanada Lakes in Wrangell-St. Elias National Park and Preserve. Wrangell-St. Elias National Park and Preserve, National Park Service., Glennallen, AK.

NPS. 1998. Resources Management Plan. Wrangell-St. Elias National Park and Preserve, Copper Center, AK.

NPS. 2003. Glacier Bay National Park and Preserve, Alaska, Vessel Quotas and Operating Requirements Final Environmental Impact Statement. National Park Service, Alaska Region, United States Department of the Interior.

NPS. 2005. Wrangell-St. Elias National Park and Preserve webpage. *in*. NPS, http://www.nps.gov/wrst.

NPS. n.d. 1985-1992. Sudden Stream Drilling Mud Removal Program. Central Alaska Network Inventory and Monitoring Program Metadata Summary Report - Wrangell-St. Elias National Park and Preserve. (www1.nature.nps.gov/im/units/ cakn/Documents/WRST_MetadataSummary.pdf). Last accessed: July 5, 2005

NPS. n.d. 1988. 1988 Sudden Stream Drilling Muds Effects on Vegetation. Central Alaska Network Inventory and Monitoring Program Metadata Summary Report - Wrangell-St. Elias National Park and Preserve. (www1.nature.nps.gov/im/units/ cakn/Documents/WRST_MetadataSummary.pdf). Last accessed: June 28, 2005

Niebauer, H. J. 1988. Effects of El Nino-Southern Oscillation and North Pacific weather patterns on interannual variability in the subarctic Bering Sea. Journal of Geophysical Research 93:5051-5068.

Oswood, M. W., A. M. Milner, and J. G. I. Irons. 1992. Climate change and Alaskan rivers and streams. Pages 192-210 in F. a. Fisher, editor. Global Climate Change and Freshwater Ecosystems. Springer-Verlag, New York.

Overpeck, J. et al. 1997. Arctic environmental change of the last four centuries. Science 278:1251-1256.

Pacyna, E. G., and J. M. Pacyna. 2002. Global emission of mercury from anthropogenic sources in 1995. Water, Air, and Soil Pollution **137**:149-165.

Patten, S. M., Jr. 1981. Seasonal Use of Coastal Habitat from Yakutat Bay to Cape Fairweather by Migratory Seabirds, Shorebirds, and Waterfowl. U.S. Department of Commerce and U.S. Department of Interior, Juneau, AK.

Paul, L. 1988. Situk River flood plain analysis. US Department of Agriculture, Forest Service, Alaska Region. R10-MB-30.

Petersen, G., A. Iverfeldt, and J. Munthe. 1995. Atmospheric mercury species over Central & Northern Europe, 1987 and 1988. Atmospheric Environment **29**:47-67.

Pilgrim, W., L. Poissant, and L. Trip. 2000. The northeast states and eastern Canadian provinces mercury study: a framework for action: summary of the Canadian chapter. The Science of the Total Environment **261**.

Powell, J., D. D'Amore, R. Thompson, T. Brock, P. Huberth, B. Bigelow, and M. T. Walter. 2003. Functional HGM wetland assessment guidebook. State of Alaska Department of Environmental Conservation, Juneau, AK.

Racine, C. H., and G. M. Ahlstrand. 1985. Response of Tussock-Shrub Terrain to Experimental All-Terrain Vehicle Tests in Wrangell-St. Elias National Park and Preserve, Alaska. Progress Report. National Park Service. Alaska Regional Office., Anchorage, AK.

Racine, C. H., and G. M. Ahlstrand. 1991. Thaw Response of Tussock-Shrub Tundra to Experimental All-Terrain Vehicle Disturbances in South-Central Alaska. Arctic **44**:31-37.

Reed, R.K. and J.D. Schumacher. 1986. Physical oceanography. Pages 57-75 in D.W. Hood and S. T. Zimmerman, editors. The Gulf of Alaska Physical Environment and Biological Resources. Alaska Office, Ocean Assessments Division, National Oceanic and Atmospheric Administration, U.S. Department of Commerce, Washington, D.C.

Reed, P. B. 1988. National list of plant species that occur in wetlands: Alaska (Region A). US Fish and Wildlife Service Biological Report 88 (26.11).

Roots, E. F. 1989. Climate Change: High latitude regions. Climate Change **15**:223-253.

Royer, T. C. 1998. Coastal Processes in the northern North Pacific. Pages 395-414 in K. H. Brink, editor. The Sea. John Wiley and Sons, NY.

Sauber, J., G.Plafker, B. F. Molnia, and M. A. Bryant. 2000. Crustal deformation associated with glacial fluctuations in eastern Chugach Mountains, Alaska. Journal Geophysical Research **105**:8055-8077.

Sauber, J., B. Plafker, B. F. Molnia, and M. A. Bryant. 2005. Elevation change (2000-2004) on the Malaspina Glacier, Alaska. European Geosciences Union, Geophysical Research Abstracts, Vol. 7.

Schindler, D. 1999. From acid rain to toxic snow. Ambio **28**:352-355.

Schroeder, W. H., and J. Munthe. 1988. Atmospheric mercury - An overview. Atmospheric Environment **32**:809-822.

Schumacher, J.D., P.J. Stebeno, and S.J. Bogard. 1993. Characteristics of an eddy over the continental shelf: Shelikof Strait, Alaska. Journal of Geophysical Research. 98:8,395-8,404.

Sease, J. L., and R. L. Loughlin. 1997. Status and population trends of Steller sea lions. Pages 22-30 *in* G. Stone, J. Goebel, and S. Webster, editors. Pinniped populations, eastern North Pacific: status, trends and issues. American Fisheries Society, Montery, CA. US Department of Commerce, NOAA Technical Memorandum, NMFS-AFSC-122, Seattle, WA.

Serreze, M. C., J. E. Walsh, F. S. C. III, T. Osterkamp, M. Dyergerov, V. Romanovsky, W. C. Oechel, J. Morison, T. Zhang, and R. G. Barry. 2000. Observational evidence of recent change in the northern high latitude environment. Climate Change **46**:159-207.

Sidle, R. C., and A. M. Milner. 1989. Stream Development in Glacier Bay National-Park, Alaska, USA. Arctic and Alpine Research **21**:350-363.

Sinclair, A. F., and W. R. Crawford. 2005. Incorporating an environmental stock-recruitment relationship in the assessment of Pacific cod (*Gadus macrocephalus*). Fisheries Oceanography 14:138-150.

Stabeno, P. J., N. A. Bond, A. J. Hermann, N. B. Kachel, C. W. Mordy, and J. E. Overland. 2004. Meteorology and oceanography of the Northern Gulf of Alaska. Continental Shelf Research **24**:859-897.

Strand, A., and O. Hov. 1996. A model strategy for the simulation of chlorinated hydrocarbon distribution in the global environment. Water, Air, Soil Pollution **86**:283-316.

Sweeney, B. W., J. K. Jackson, D. Newbold, and D. H. Funk. 1992. Climate change and the life histories and biogeography of aquatic insects in eastern North America. Pages 143-176 *in* F. a. Fisher, editor. Global Climate Change and Freshwater Ecosystems. Springer-Verlag, New York.

Thompson, M. 1997. Case Incident Record, Malaspina Forelands/Esker Stream. United States Department of the Interior, National Park Service.

Trabant, D. C., R. M. Krimmel, K. A. Echelmeyer, S. L. Zirnheld, and D. H. Elsberg. 2003a. The slow advance of a calving glacier: Hubbard Glacier, Alaska, USA. Annals of Glaciology, Vol 36 **36**:45-50.

Trabant, D. C., R. S. March, and D. S. Thomas. 2003b. Hubbard Glacier, Alaska: Growing and Advancing in Spite of Global Climate Change and the 1986 and 2002 Russell Lake Outburst Floods. US Geological Survey Fact Sheet 001-03.

US Census Bureau. 2000. Profile of General Demographic Characteristics: 2000. Geographic Area: Yakutat City and Borough, Alaska. http://censtats.census.gov/data/AK/05002282.pdf. Last accessed: June 24, 2005

US Department of the Interior. 1992. Geological Report for the Gulf of Alaska Planning Area, MMS 92-0065. U.S. Department of the Interior, Minerals Management Service, Alaska OCS Region.

USFWS. 2003. National Wetlands Inventory Status - Alaska. http://wetlands.fws.gov/reg7webstat.gif. Last accessed: July 6, 2005

Walter, M. T. 2003. Final Report: Lemon Creek Natural Sediment Assessment. Alaska Department of Environmental Conservation ACWA Program, Anchorage, AK.

Walter, M. T., E. Neal, and C. Byers. 2004. Duck Creek is dying: Evidence that uplift may by one of the killers. *in* Geological Society of America Annual Meeting, Seattle, WA.

Wania, F., and D. Mackay. 1996. Tracking the distribution of persistent organic pollutants. Environmental Science and Technology **30**:390A-396A.

Wania, F., D. Mackay, Y.-F. Li, T. F. Bidleman, and A. Strand. 1999. Global chemical fate of α-hexachlorocyclohexane. 1. Evaluation of a global distribution model. Environmental Toxicology and Chemistry **18**:1390-1399.

Webster, J. R., and E. F. Benfield. 1986. Vascular plant breakdown in freshwater ecosystems. Annual Review of Ecology and Systematics **17**:567-594.

Weeks, D. P. 2003. Wrangell - St. Elias National Park and Preserve Alaska Water Resources Scoping Report. US Department of the Interior, National Park Service, Water Resources Division, Denver, CO.

Weingartner, T.J., S.L. Danielson, and T.C. Royer. 2005. Freshwater variability and predictability in the Alaska Coastal Current. Deep Sea Research II. 52: 169-191.

Williams, P. 1989. Adapting water resources management to global climate change. Climate Change **15**.

Wilson, J.G. and J.E. Overland. 1986. Meterology. In D.W. Hood and S.T. Zimmerman Eds. The Gulf of Alaska: Physical Environment and Biological Resources. NOAA Ocean Assessment Division, Alaska Office, Washington, D.C.

Willson, M. F., S. M. Gende, and B. H. Marston. 1998. Fishes and the forest: expanding perspectives on fish-wildlife interactions. Bio Science:445-462.

Wipfli, M. S., J. Hudson, and J. Caouette. 1998. Influence of salmon carcasses on stream productivity: response of biofilm and benthic macroinvertebrates in southeastern Alaska, USA. Canadian Journal of Fisheries and Aquatic Sciences **55**:1503-1511.

Appendices

Appendix A. Seabirds, marine mammals and sharks surveyed in the Malaspina Forelands section of coastal WRST (Kozie 1993).

Common Name	Species
Birds	
Pacific Loon	*Gavia pacifica*
Common Loon	*Gavia immer*
Unidentified Albatross	*Diomedea spp*
Northern Fulmar	*Fulmarus glacialis*
Short-tailed Shearwater	*Puffinus tenuirostris*
Double-crested Cormorant	*Phalacrocorax auritus*
Pelagic Cormorant	*Phalacrocorax pelagicus*
Canada Goose	*Branta canadensis*
Mallard	*Anas platyrhynchos*
Northern Shoveler	*Anas clypeata*
Harlequin Duck	*Histrionicus histrionicus*
Surf Scoter	*Melanitta perspicillata*
White-winged Scoter	*Melanitta fusca*
Unidentified Scoter	*Melanitta spp*
Barrow's Goldeneye	*Bucephala islandica*
Common Merganser	*Mergus merganser*
Red-breasted Merganser	*Mergus serrator*
Osprey	*Pandion haliaetus*
Bald Eagle	*Haliaeetus leucocephalus*
Peregrine Falcon	*Falco peregrinus*
Semipalmated Plover	*Charadrius semipalmatus*
Black Oystercatcher	*Haematopus bachmani*
Spotted Sandpiper	*Actitis macularia*
Whimbrel	*Numenius phaeopus*
Ruddy Turnstone	*Arenaria interpres*
Black Turnstone	*Arenaria melanocephala*
Sanderling	*Calidris alba*
Western Sandpiper	*Calidris mauri*
Least Sandpiper	*Calidris minutilla*
Short-billed Dowitcher	*Limnodromus griseus*
Red-necked Phalarope	*Phalaropus lobatus*
Unidentified Shorebird	*Scolopacidae (Family)*
Pomarine Jaeger	*Stercorarius pomarinus*
Parasitic Jaeger	*Stercorarius parasiticus*
Bonaparte's Gull	*Larus philadelphia*
Mew Gull	*Larus canus*
Herring Gull	*Larus argentatus*

Glaucous-winged Gull	*Larus glaucescens*
Unidentified Gull	*Larus and/or Rissa spp*
Black-legged Kittiwake	*Rissa tridactyla*
Arctic Tern	*Sterna paradisaea*
Aleutian Tern	*Sterna aleutica*
Common Murre	*Uria aalge*
Pigeon Guillemot	*Cepphus columba*
Marbled Murrelet	*Brachyramphus marmoratus*
Kittlitz's Murrelet	*Brachyramphus brevirostris*
Unidentified Murrelet	*Brachyramphus spp*
Ruby-throated Hummingbird	*Archilochus colubris*
Bank Swallow	*Riparia riparia*
Unidentified Swallow	*Hirundinidae (Family)*
Black-billed Magpie	*Pica pica*
Northwestern Crow	*Corvus caurinus*
Savannah Sparrow	*Passerculus sandwichensis*
Marine Mammals	
Harbor Seal	*Phoca vitulina*
Elephant Seal	*Mirounga angustirostris*
Steller Sea Lion	*Eumetopias jubatus*
Sea Otter	*Enhydra lutris*
Harbor Porpoise	*Phocoena phocoena*
Humpback Whale	*Megaptera novaeangliae*
Minke Whale	*Balaenoptera acutorostrata*
Fish	
Basking Shark	*Cetorhinus maximus*

Appendix B. Plant species found at the Icy Bay Mine Site, along west Icy Bay. This species list taken from Cook (1990).

Common Name	Taxon	Wetland Status
Trees		
Sitka spruce	Picea sitchensis	
Black cottonwood	Populus balsamifera subsp. trichocarpa	
Shrubs		
Red baneberry	Actaea rubra	
Goatsbeard	Aruncus Sylvester	
Feltleaf willow	Salix alaxensis	
Hooker willow	Salix hookeriana	
Sitka willow	Salix sitchensis	
Forbs		
Common yarrow	Achillea borealis	
Pearly everlasting	Anaphalis margaritacea	
Angelica	Angelica lucida	
Lyrate rock cress	Arabis lyrata	
Aster	Aster subspicatus	
Broom rape	Boschiniakia rossica	
Bluejoint	Calamagrostis Canadensis subsp. Langsdorffii	
Broad-leaf marsh marigold	Caltha biflora	OW
Beringian chickweed	Cerastium Beeringianum var. grandiflorum	
Hemlock parsley	Conioselinum chinense	FW
Swedish cornel	Cornus suedica	
Glandular willow herb	Epilobium glandulosum	
River beauty	Epilobium latifolium	
Willow herb	Epilobium leptocarpum	FW
Beach strawberry	Fragaria chiloensis	
Small bedstraw	Galium trifidum	FW
Large-leaf avens	Geum macrophyllum	
Common marestail	Hippuris vulgaris	OW
Seabeach sandwort	Honckenya peploides	OW
Beach pea	Lathyrus maritimus	
Beach lovage	Ligusticum scoticum	
Nootkaten lupine	Lupinus nootkatensis	
Northern grass-of-parnassus	Parnassia palustris	FW
White bog orchis	Platanthera dilate	FW
Liverleaf wintergreen	Pyrola asarifolia	
One-sided wintergreen	Pyrola secunda	
Yellow rattle	Rhinanthus arcticus	
Marsh yellow cress	Rorippa islandica	
Western dock	Rumex fenestratus	FW
Ditch grass	Ruppia spiralis	OW

Snow pearlwort	Sagina intermedia	
Star-flower Solomon's seal	Smilacina stellata	
	Stellaria calycantha	
	Stellaria humifusa	FW
Long-leaved starwort	Stellaria longifolia	
Graminoids		
Wheat grass	Agropyron violaceum subsp. andinum	
Tickle grass	Agrostis scabra	
Blue joint	Calamagrostis Canadensis	
Sedge	Carex Kelloggii	OW
Sedge	Carex Lyngbyaei	OW
Mertens sedge	Carex Mertensii	FW
Berine hairgrass	Deschampsia beringensis	
Hairgrass	Deschampsia sp.	
Creeping spikerush	Eleocharis palustris	OW
Dune grass	Elymus arenarius	
Red fescue	Festuca rubra	
Red fescue	Festuca rubra subsp. aucata	
	Festuca sp.	
Squirreltail grass	Hordeum jubatum	
Alpine rush	Juncus alpinus	OW
Arctic rush	Juncus arcticus subsp. sitchensis	OW
Chestnut rush	Juncus castaneus subsp. castaneus	FW
Many-flowered wood rush	Luzula multiflora	
Timothy grass	Phleum commutatum	
Arctic bluegrass	Poa actica subsp. Williamsii	
Bluegrass	Poa sp.	
Marsh arrow grass	Triglochin palustris	OW
Lower vasculars		
Meadow horsetail	Equisetum arvense	
Swamp horsetail	Equisetum fluviatile	OW
Meadow horsetail	Equisetum pretense	FW
Fir club moss	Lycopodium selago	
Mosses		
	Rhacomitrium canenscens	
	Rhytidium rogosum	

OW = Obligate wetland species. Occurs almost always under natural conditions in wetlands (Reed 1988). FW = Facultative wetland species. Usually occurs in wetlands but occasionally found in nonwetlands.

Appendix C. Plant species found in a vegetative survey of the east Sitkagi Bluffs of the Malaspina Forelands (NPS 1990).

Common Name	Taxon	Wetland Status
Trees		
Sitka spruce	Picea sitchensis	
Black cottonwood	Populus balsamifera subsp. trichocarpa	
Shrubs		
Red baneberry	Picea sitchensis	
Sitka alder	Alnus cruspa subsp. sinuate	
Devil's club	Echinopanax horridum	
Salmonberry	Rubus spectabilis	
Forbs		
Common yarrow	Achillea borealis	
Angelica	Angelica lucida	
Indian paintbrush	Castilleja chrymactis	
Unalaska Indian paintbrush	Castilleja unalaschcensis	
Hemlock parsley	Conioselinum chinense	FW
Northern coral root	Corallorrhiza trifida	FW
Fireweed	Epilobium angustifolium	
Beach strawberry	Fragaria chiloensis	
Cow parsnip	Heracleum lanatum	
Seabeach sandwort	Honckenya peploides	OW
Beach pea	Lathyrus maritimus	
Beach loveage	Ligusticum scoticum	
Twayblade	Listera cordata	
Nootkaten lupine	Lupinus nootkatensis	
Single delight	Monenses uniflora	
Liverleaf wintergreen	Pyrola asarifolia	
One-sided wintergreen	Pyrola secunda	
Star-flower Solomon's seal	Smilacina stellata	
Lace flower	Tiarella trifoliate	
Graminoids		
Sedge	Carex Kelloggii	OW
Dune grass	Elymus arenarius	
Red fescue	Festuca rubra	
Small-flowered woodrush	Luzula parviflora	
Glaucous bluegrass	Poa glauca	
Lower Vasculars		
Lady fern	Athyrium filix-femina	
Meadow horsetail	Equisetum arvense	
Oak fern	Gymnnocarpium dryopteris	

Mosses		
	Cratoneuron sp.	
	Dicranum sp.	
	Polytrichum commune	
	Polytrichum sp.	
	Rhizomnium glabrescens	
	Rhytidiadelphus loreus	
Liverworts		
	Plagiochila asplenoides	
Lichens		
	Nephroma sp.	
	Peltigera polydactyla	

OW = Obligate wetland species. Occurs almost always under natural conditions in wetlands (Reed 1988). FW = Facultative wetland species. Usually occurs in wetlands but occasionally found in nonwetlands.

Appendix D. Selected water quality standards for the State of Alaska Standards for all parameters except fecal coliform bacteria refer to the criteria for the "Growth and Propagation of Fish, Shellfish, Other Aquatic Life, and Wildlife". Fecal Coliform bacteria refers to the "Water Recreation – contact recreation" criterion (ADEC 2003).

Parameter	Criteria
Fresh Water Standards	
Fecal Coliform Bacteria (FC)	In a 30-day period, the geometric mean of samples may not exceed 100FC/100 ml, and not more than one sample, or more than 10% of the samples if there are more than 10 samples, may exceed 200FC/100 ml.
Dissolved Gas	Dissolved Oxygen (D.O.) must be greater than 7 mg/L in waters used by anadramous or resident fish. In no case may D.O. be less than 5 mg/L to a depth of 20 in the interstitial waters of gravel used by anadramous or resident fish for spawning. For waters not used by anadramous or resident fish, D.O. must be greater than or equal to 5 mg/L. In no case may D.O. be greater than 17 mg/L or exceed 110% of saturation.
Dissolved Inorganic Substances	Total dissolved solids (TDS) may not exceed 1,000 mg/L. A concentration of TDS may not be present in water if that concentration causes or could reasonably be expected to cause an adverse effect to aquatic life.
Petroleum, Hydrocarbons, Oils and Grease	Total aqueous hydrocarbons (TAqH) in the water column may not exceed 15μg/L. total aromatic hydrocarbons (TAH) in water may not exceed 10 μg/L. There may be no concentrations of petroleum hydrocarbons, animal fats, or vegetable oils in shoreline or bottom sediments that cause deleterious effects to aquatic life. Surface waters and adjoining shorelines must be virtually free from floating oil, film, sheen, or discoloration.
pH	May not be less than 6.5 or greater than 8.5. May not vary more than 0.5 pH units outside of the naturally occurring range.

Sediment	The percent accumulation of fine sediment (0.1-4.0 mm) in the spawning grounds of anadramous or resident fish may not be increased more than 5% by weight above natural conditions. In no case may the fine sediment range in those gravel beds exceed a maximum of 30% by weight (as shown from grain size accumulation graph). In all other surface waters, no sediment loads (suspended or deposited) that can cause adverse effects on aquatic animal or plant life, their reproduction or habitat may be present.
Temperature	May not exceed 20°C at any time. The following maximum temperatures may not be exceeded, where applicable: **Migration routes** 15°C **Spawning areas** 13°C **Rearing areas** 15°C **Egg and fry incubation** 13°C For all other waters, the weekly average temperature may not exceed site-specific requirements needed to preserve normal species diversity or to prevent the appearance of nuisance organisms.
Turbidity	May not exceed 25 nephelometric turbidity units (NTU) above natural conditions. For all lake waters, may not exceed 5 NTU above natural conditions.
Marine Water Standards	
Fecal Coliform Bacteria (FC)	Same as fresh water standard.
Dissolved Gas	Surface dissolved oxygen concentration in coastal water may not be less than 6.0 mg/L for a depth of one meter except when natural conditions cause this value to be depressed. D.O. may not be reduced below 4 mg/L at any point beneath the surface. D.O. concentrations in estuaries and tidal tributaries may not be less than 5.0 mg/L except where natural conditions cause this value to be depressed. In no case may D.O. levels exceed 17 mg/L. the concentration of total dissolved gas may not exceed 100% of saturation.
Dissolved Inorganic Substances	Maximum allowable variation above natural salinity (parts per thousand): **Natural** **Human-Induced**

	Salinity	Salinity
	0.0 to 3.5	1
	Greater than 3.5 to 13.5	2
	Greater than 13.5 to 35.0	4
Petroleum, Hydrocarbons, Oils and Grease	Same as fresh water standard.	
pH	May not be less than 6.5 or greater than 8.5. May not vary more than 0.2 pH units outside of the naturally occurring range.	
Sediment	No measurable increase in concentration of settable solids above natural conditions, as measured by the volumetric Imhoff cone method.	
Temperature	May not cause the weekly average temperature to increase more than 1C. the maximum rate of change may not exceed 0.5C per hour. Normal daily temperature cycles may not be altered in amplitude or frequency.	
Turbidity	May not reduce the depth of the compensation point for photosynthetic activity by more than 10%. May not reduce the maximum secchi disk depth by more than 10%.	

The Alaska Water Quality Standards specify the degree of degradation that may not be exceeded in a waterbody as a result of human actions (ADEC 2003). The Alaska Water Quality Standards designate specific uses for which water quality must be protected, and specifies the pollutant limits, or criteria, necessary to protect these uses.

There are seven designated uses for fresh waters, and seven designated uses for marine waters specified in the Alaska Water Quality Standards (ADEC 2003). The seven freshwater uses are: drinking water; agriculture; aquaculture; industrial; contact recreation; non-contact recreation; and growth and propagation of fish, shellfish, other aquatic life, and wildlife. The seven marine water uses are: aquaculture; seafood processing; industrial; contact recreation; non-contact recreation; growth and propagation of fish, shellfish, other aquatic life, and wildlife; and harvesting for consumption of raw mollusks or other raw aquatic life. For each of these uses, the Alaska Water Quality Standards specify criteria for a variety of parameters or pollutants, which are both numeric and descriptive (ADEC 2003). According to the federal Clean Water Act Section 305(b) and Section 303(d), waterbodies are compared to the criteria for these parameters to determine if persistent water quality violations occur, and if so into which status category waterbodies are listed.

Appendix E. Non-indigenous invasive species that have invaded or could soon invade Southeast Alaska. The species listed are all highly invasive, have caused severe impact in areas they have spread to, and are capable of living in Alaska's climate. Many of these species have already spread to the Pacific Northwest and are a risk to Alaska. From ADFG (2002a).

Species	Originally from...	Now located in...	Why it is a concern
Fish:			
Northern Pike	Alaska	Spreading to other areas of Alaska	Highest priority threat to Southcentral Alaska. They eliminate or greatly reduce the native species. Cause damage to resident species (rainbow trout and grayling). Potential impact to coho salmon stocks.
Atlantic Salmon	Escape from Fish farms in BC and Washington	Cordova Ketchikan Yakutat Bering Sea	Serious threat to native species due to competition in stream habitat. Displace native fish by out-competing for food and spawning habitat.
Yellow perch		Kenai Peninsula	Compete with all resident fish species and salmon fry. This population has been eradicated.
Ornamental aquarium fish			Compete with and may feed on native species.
Invertebrates:			
Green crab	N. Europe	California to Vancouver Island	Out-competes resident species for shoreline habitat. Very aggressive.
New Zealand mud snail	New Zealand	Europe Asia Idaho Montana Wyoming California Arizona	May impact the food chain for native trout and the physical characteristics of streams themselves. A serious threat to Alaska's sport fisheries.
Chinese mitten crab	China	San Francisco Bay/delta Possible it is in Oregon's Columbia River	Similar life history to American eel and can move upriver hundreds of miles displacing native species. Feeds on salmonid eggs.
Zebra mussel	Europe	Great Lakes	Out-compete resident mussels, clog water intake lines, sequester nutrients for primary production.
Signal crayfish	W. Canada	Kodiak Island	Out-compete stream fauna, eat everything, can survive extended periods of drought and famine.
Spiny water flea	Europe	Great Lakes California	Displaces existing zooplankton communities but is unpalatable to fish resulting in lower fish numbers.
Parasites:			
Whirling disease	Eurasian continent	Present in 22 states. Found in all western states except Arizona and Alaska.	Parasitic infection that attacks juvenile trout and salmon. Causes fish to swim erratically and in severe cases, to die.
Plants:			

Hydrilla or water thyme	Originally from S. India and Korea.	Present in 15 states including California and Washington	Hydrilla is a noxious water weed that can quickly spread to become an impenetrable mat. Fills lakes and rivers completely until i "tops out" at the surface. Native plants are out-competed. Greatly slows water flow and clogs the area. Can alter water chemistry and oxygen levels. Hinders fish development.
Dotted duckweed	Australia and Southeast Asia	Present in 22 states including Oregon	This small floating plant grows rapidly into dense masses in still water covering the entire surface in a green "bloom".
Purple loosestrife	Eurasia	Present in all states except Hawaii and Alaska Also found in Canada.	Loosestrife is able to rapidly establish and replace native vegetation with a dense, homogeneous stand that reduces local biodiversity, endangers rare species and provides little value to wildlife.
Eurasian water-milfoil	Europe and North Africa	Present in 46 states including Alaska	Found in a variety of habits, becoming established in both impoundments and natural waters, sometimes brackish water or in clear, cool, spring-fed rivers. Problems include displacement of native vegetation, disruption of navigation and recreation by the formation of impenetrable mats, and decreased water flow.
Reed Canary grass	Eurasia	All but the southeastern portion of the US including Alaska. Also found in Canada.	Is invading freshwater wetlands and in some places choking channels of small streams. It creeping rhizomes out-compete native grasses leading to less biodiversity.
Japanese knotweed	Great Britain	Sitka Juneau Other Southeast Alaska areas	Spreads rapidly, choking out native plants. Can spread along streambanks, shorelines, and estuaries. Loss of springtime cover and woody streamside vegetation causes destabilized stream banks and less woody debris in streams.
Foxtail barley	Western North America	Juneau Interior Alaska	Invades salt marsh habitats
Salt marsh cordgrass	Eastern seaboard of the US from Maine to Texas	Has spread to Canada and western US including Washington, Oregon, and California.	Able to trap sediment leading to higher deposition rates. Changes water circulation patterns. Competitive replacement of native plants and impacts native flora and fauna in intertidal zone. Also, decreases production o bottom-dwelling algae, changes bottom-dwelling invertebrate populations, and loss o shorebird foraging areas.
Dense-flowered cordgrass	Chile South America	California	Outcompetes native flora and impacts native fauna. Eliminates foraging habitat for shorebirds and waterfowl. Dense clusters slo the flow of water and increase sedimentation (raising the wetland).
Swollen bladderwort	Southeastern US	Western Washington	Grows in still or slow-moving water and forms dense beds of floating plants. Impacts native plants and animals and water quality.

As the nation's principal conservation agency, the Department of the Interior has responsibility for most of our nationally owned public lands and natural resources. This includes fostering sound use of our land and water resources; protecting our fish, wildlife, and biological diversity; preserving the environmental and cultural values of our national parks and historical places; and providing for the enjoyment of life through outdoor recreation. The department assesses our energy and mineral resources and works to ensure that their development is in the best interests of all our people by encouraging stewardship and citizen participation in their care. The department also has a major responsibility for American Indian reservation communities and for people who live in island territories under U.S. administration.

NPS D-90, January 2006